Develop the Mindset
of an
Attitude of Gratitude

ROGER GRAY

WITH

RODNEY GRAY

Copyright © 2014 Roger Gray and Rodney Gray

All rights reserved

~~~~ ~~~~

Cover Art by Nathalie Kelley

Paperback-Press
an imprint of A & S Publishing
A & S Holmes, Inc.

ISBN: 0692314393
ISBN-13: 978-0692314395

CONTENTS

ACKNOWLEDGMENTS

First, I want to thank God for enabling and allowing me to pen these words. As I write this there is a small voice in my head that says, "You are going to blame God for this feeble effort?" Yes, as humble a work as it is I could not have done it without His inspiration. And if one person receives ten percent as much help and growth from it as I did in writing it, it was worth every bit of the effort. Thank you God!

Secondly, thanks to my son Rod. Without his help and encouragement it would not have been completed. He is the writer in the family. His council on the technical aspects of writing and his knowledge of grammar were invaluable. There were times I was tempted to discard the project. During those times Rod and his wife Ina offered words of encouragement that motivated me to continue. Thank you Rod and Ina!

Thirdly, I'm grateful to Dr. Robert A. Emmons at UC, Davis, for his research on gratitude for the past fourteen years. There are many others who followed in that work since 2000, but Emmons was the pioneer in the field. Thanks Dr. Emmons for your research and the books you have written.

Fourth, thanks to my children and their mother who lived with me through my crazy years: Karen, Rod, Wes, Tera and Barbara, through it all they loved and forgave me. Thank you guys!

Fifth, I offer much gratitude to Sharon Kizziah-

Holmes, publishing coordinator of Paperback-Press publishing. Without Sharon's help this book would not have become a reality!

Sixth, thanks to Nathalie Kelly, the very talented illustrator who designed the cover for this book!

Seventh, thanks to everyone that has crossed my path since day one of this life, the good, bad and ugly. All of it has contributed to who I am today. And for that and them I'm very grateful!

PREFACE

I have known a few people (I'm sure you have known some like them) whom it didn't matter the news they received, their response was always the same: " Thank you Lord." or " Praise the Lord." It could be good news or bad news: they always gave the same response.   I used to find that very irritating.

In the past few years I have learned that those people knew something I had not yet learned. They had learned to obey God! In 1 Thessalonians 5:18, Paul tells us, "In all things give thanks for this is the will of God in Christ Jesus concerning you." In all things--not just the good things--give thanks. Whether everyone is for us or the whole world is against us, give God thanks.

I can't but wonder how different my life would have been if I had learned this principle 45 years ago. God has been dealing with me in this matter for some time. I have been such a slow learner. It has been a process or a journey.

I invite you to join me on this journey. The objective is to grow in Christ-likeness until we develop a mindset that causes us to respond to whatever comes into our life with a heart-felt attitude of gratitude. To do so is an act of obedience to God and can only be the result of total trust in Him.

Adam Clark in his commentary writes in reference to 1 Thessalonians 5:18, "For gratitude and obedience are inseparably connected."[*1]

In the early 70's I was very happy in what I was doing and knew that I would be pastoring for the rest of my life. There is a certain kind of security in knowing what your purpose in life is and to know you are going to be doing that for the rest of your life. Then something happens to change all of that. I don't think it's necessary to go into all the details, but I made a decision that I felt was in the best interest of my family, a decision to request to be relocated to another church. The hierarchy stated that I would stay or I would never pastor another church. There was only one person on earth that could change that, my district superintendent. He was close to my situation and had offered another church, but before it was all settled he died from a heart attack.

So there I was, the rug pulled out from under me: can't fulfill my purpose, can't practice my profession. I had a wife and four young children that I was responsible for. What could I do? I should have had an attitude of gratitude, but I didn't.

Did I believe that God could override the hierarchy? Certainly! Did I believe that God could have healed the district superintendent? Certainly! But he didn't and I became very angry at Him. This kind of anger leads to a battle that we will lose every time, but that was the battle I kept fighting off and on for many years. If only I had been mature enough in my walk with Jesus Christ to trust Him and had an attitude of gratitude, my life would have been so much different.

Now don't misunderstand, my life has not been all that bad, but I feel that I have not totally fulfilled my purpose. And more importantly I have hurt a lot of people, not on purpose but as result of my rebellion against God. You have to be crazy to try to do battle with God and as a result you are going to act crazy at times. It was during those times that I hurt others and especially those closest to me.

If you are reading this book and have been hurt by me, from the very depths of my heart I ask your forgiveness. I hope and pray that you found God's grace sufficient to carry you through the disappointment and hurt and that your life has been richly blessed by God.

All I can do is say to God: "I'm sorry. Please forgive me." I assure you I have begged His forgiveness a thousand times. I know he has forgiven, but I don't always feel it and the truth is, I have a harder time forgiving myself.

I know as I mature in Christ-likeness and develop the mindset that responds with total trust in Him in all aspects of life, I will feel total forgiveness. I also know that I can't even imagine the blessings He has in store as I develop that attitude of gratitude. Thank you for joining me in this adventure!

INTRODUCTION

This is not an attempt to present a concept or ritual whereby we can manipulate God to give us all the toys we desire. God can't and will not be manipulated; however, He has already provided blessings "exceedingly abundantly above all that we ask or think." (Ephesians 3:20) Developing a mindset of an attitude of gratitude moves us into position to receive those blessings.

I want to boil some tea, or in my case water, for my instant oatmeal. Ugh, nasty stuff, but they say it is good for you. Anyway the teakettle is empty; I take the lid off, leave the teakettle on the range but turn the water faucet on and let it run. After five minutes I wonder why the teakettle is not full. The answer is obvious: I have to move the teakettle under the water faucet. God's blessings are flowing like the water from the faucet, or more like an artesian well. We need to move into the flow. Developing a mindset of an attitude of gratitude will keep us in the flow of God's blessing.

Develop the Mindset of an Attitude of Gratitude

Definition of the title

Let's define what we mean by developing the mindset of an attitude of gratitude. So often we use words without thinking of their meaning, thus losing the impact of the message. Consider the dictionary definition of each of these words: Mindset: an attitude, deposition, mood, inclination, fixed response; Attitude: a mental posture or position taken toward an event or circumstance; Gratitude: giving thanks, thanksgiving, the act of being grateful.

Let's sum this up in this way; Our challenge is to develop the habitual response of taking a mental posture of thanksgiving toward any event or circumstance in our lives. Most of us respond from a negative mindset towards events and circumstances in our lives. Thus we respond with worry, fret and/or anger. It is a habit that we should want to change. Perhaps the easiest way to change a habit is to replace it with a new one. Thus developing the mindset of an attitude of gratitude.

It does not happen overnight, it is a process, or journey. It is a journey that will not end until that day we look into the face of Jesus with hearts bursting with love and gratitude and say from the very depth of our being, THANK YOU! And that will be a new beginning rather than an end.

Attitude:

Let's take a little deeper look at attitude, the mental posture we adopt toward any event or circumstance in our life. The mental posture we adopt in any situation is our choice. Dr. Viktor Frankl writes in *Man's Search for Meaning*, "Everything can be taken from a man but one thing; the last of the human freedoms; to choose one's attitude in any given set of circumstances."[*1] This philosophy was not developed in an ivory tower, but rather by spending six plus years in Nazi concentration camps.

Dr. Frankl survived through a series of miracles. It was largely due to the fact that he endeavored to be grateful for his past life, his hope for a future life and seeking out what beauty could be found in his dire circumstances such as a beautiful sunrise or sunset.

Regardless of how bleak our situation might seem, we have that same freedom and right: to choice our attitude. We can choose to worry and fret; to be resentful, bitter, or vengeful; or to be grateful. Choosing to be grateful will totally change your situation and life: "In all things give thanks for this is the will of God in Christ Jesus."(I Thessalonians 5:18)

CHAPTER ONE

How Grateful Am I?

I have heard it said or have read some place that a successful sermon gives the worshippers something to think about, something to feel and something to do. That is the criteria that we have set for this book. We want you involved in developing a stronger mindset of an attitude of gratitude. To achieve that objective we are including some gratitude exercises.

First, let's take a mental inventory of our present mindset or habit of reacting to stimuli we receive moment by moment throughout the day. You may want to jot down some of the surprises you learn in this process. Many of us who consider ourselves to have a positive mental attitude may be surprised at our initial reaction to some stimuli. Remember, our objective on this journey is to grow until our response to all stimuli is always one of gratitude. Will we reach that objective? Probably not in this lifetime, but we will improve in ways that will make an unbelievable difference in our lives.

Let's start with checking our self-talk. We talk to ourselves continuously; most of the time we are unaware of it and certainly unaware of what we are saying. This self-talk affects our feelings, thoughts, and behavior. It reflects our true self-image. Those of us that spend a lot of time alone often verbalize our self-talk. (We don't want to admit it.) But I must confess that I find myself talking out loud to myself often. I have been shocked at some of the things that have come out of my mouth. There have been times that I have asked, "Where did that come from?" Often I have asked God for forgiveness and thanked Him for showing me something I needed to work on. Focus on this mental exercise for a few days. A couple days may be adequate for some of you and others may need a week. Most of us will find this helpful to do occasionally as we continue the journey.

Secondly, let's take a mental inventory of our nemesis to a mindset of gratitude. I suspect we all have one. I was surprised when I started paying attention to my reactions in different situations throughout the day. I call it my pet peeve. I'm not sure if my pet peeve is something I developed with age or if it has been with me all these years. But I was shocked to discover that my pet peeve is other drivers. A driver can pull out in front of me and I instantly become a totally different person. I want to give them a piece of my mind or at least wave at them with less than a handful of fingers.

There are days when I'll have my morning devotions and do my gratitude exercises and be on top of the world, full of gratitude. Then I get in my car, drive one block and some character pulls out in front of me almost causing me to rear-end him. A total transformation comes over me, forget gratitude, I need to let him know what an unsafe driver he is. Then I have to say, "Forgive me God and teach me more patience and tolerance."

I was unaware of this in myself until I started working on developing a mindset of an attitude of gratitude about three years ago. I have gotten much better with this nemesis, but I'm not perfect yet. I can identify with the title of one of author Jess Lair's books: *I Ain't Well-But I Am Sure Better*.

About 90 percent of the time I say, "Thank you God for your protection." At other times when I get upset instead of being grateful I feel like God is laughing at me and saying, "You're a slow learner, kid." This mental exercise has been very helpful to me and I'm sure many of you will find it so for you. Do this exercise for a few days. You can do it concurrently with the self-talk exercise.

Thirdly, we are including a quiz to help you see how grateful you are now.

Fourth, we suggest that you do gratitude exercises, including keeping a gratitude journal for at least four weeks.

Fifth, we suggest that after four weeks gratitude exercising you take the gratitude quiz again to see your growth in gratitude. Many of you will find that you want to make the gratitude exercising a continuing part of your life.

The following quiz was developed by Dr. Robert Emmons at the University of California, Davis campus. He has studied the subject of gratitude for over a decade, working with hundreds of people from age eight to 80. You can take this quiz on-line if you like and get feed-back from Dr. Emmon's organization. You will find this very helpful:

www.greatergood.berkeley.edu/quizzies/take_quiz/6

1. I feel very thankful for my degree of physical health.

Never
Once a year
A few times a year
Once a month
A few times a month
Once a week
More than once a week

2. I count my blessings for what I have in this world.

Never
Once a year
A few times a year
Once a month
A few times a month
Once a week
More than once a week

3. I reflect on the worst times in my life to help me realize how fortunate I am now.

Never
Once a year
A few times a year
Once a month
A few times a month
Once a week
More than once a week

4. I think of people who are less fortunate than I am to help me feel more satisfied with my circumstances.

Never
Once a year
A few times a year
Once a month
A few times a month
Once a week
More than once a week

5. I remind myself how fortunate I am to have the privileges and opportunities I have encountered in life.

Never
Once a year
A few times a year
Once a month
A few times a month
Once a week
More than once a week

6. I reflect on how fortunate I am to have basic things in life like food, clothing, and shelter.

Never
Once a year
A few times a year
Once a month
A few times a month
Once a week
More than once a week

7. I really notice and acknowledge the good things I get in life.

Never
Once a year
A few times a year
Once a month
A few times a month
Once a week
More than once a week

8. When I swerve to avoid a car accident, I feel relieved that I am ok.

Strongly Disagree
Disagree
Somewhat Disagree
Neither Agree nor Disagree
Somewhat Agree
Agree
Strongly Agree

9. I am content with what I have.

Strongly Disagree

Disagree
Somewhat Disagree
Neither Agree nor Disagree
Somewhat Agree
Agree
Strongly Agree

10. When I drive by the scene of a car accident, it reminds me to feel thankful that I am safe.

Strongly Disagree
Disagree
Somewhat Disagree
Neither Agree nor Disagree
Somewhat Agree
Agree
Strongly Agree

11. It is important to appreciate things such as health, family, and friends.

Strongly Disagree
Disagree
Somewhat Disagree
Neither Agree nor Disagree
Somewhat Agree
Agree
Strongly Agree

12. Although I don't have everything I want, I am thankful for what I have.

Strongly Disagree
Disagree
Somewhat Disagree

Neither Agree nor Disagree
Somewhat Agree
Agree
Strongly Agree

13. I remind myself to think about the good things I have in my life.
Strongly Disagree
Disagree
Somewhat Disagree
Neither Agree nor Disagree
Somewhat Agree
Agree
Strongly Agree

14. I appreciate my degree of success in life so far.
Strongly Disagree
Disagree
Somewhat Disagree
Neither Agree nor Disagree
Somewhat Agree
Agree
Strongly Agree

15. When I see someone less fortunate than myself, I realize how lucky I am.
Strongly Disagree
Disagree
Somewhat Disagree
Neither Agree nor Disagree
Somewhat Agree
Agree

Strongly Agree
Other

16. What describes your highest level of education?
Did not finish high school
High school diploma
Associate degree or certificate program
Bachelor's degree
Did some graduate study
Graduate or professional degree

17. What best describes your current employment status?
Employed
Self-employed
Stay-at-home parent
Unemployed
Student
Retired

18. How spiritual are you?
Not at all
Slightly
Somewhat
Very
Extremely [1]

The results from taking this quiz can serve as an indicator of areas you might want to focus on in your journey to developing a mindset of an attitude of gratitude. We suggest doing your gratitude exercising in the next chapter for four weeks then re-taking the quiz. This will reveal your progress and many of you will be pleasantly surprised. This will also provide motivation to continue on your gratitude journey.

CHAPTER TWO

Gratitude Exercising

For the next four weeks do gratitude exercises. Many of you will discover that you want to continue this practice, perhaps making it a part of your daily devotions. Before we get into gratitude exercising let's make a few observations about this book and gratitude.

Warning: If you apply the concepts in this book you may experience some side effects. Studies done by several different organizations over the past fourteen years and my own experiences in gratitude exercising over the past three years reveal some amazing results. The following are some of the possible side effects. You might:

1. Sleep better.
2. Release stress easier and faster.
3. Have fewer symptoms of illness.

4.   Have improved relationships at all levels.
5.   Experience more joy and happiness.
6.   Become more spiritually minded.
7.   Develop a greater faith and trust in the grace and love of God.
8.   Live a more consistent Christian life.
9.   Find your blood pressure lowered. (Do not discontinue your medication without consulting your doctor.)

I have even noticed that I feel safer when driving and consistently find convenient parking places at the supermarket, the mall and school. So read this book and apply these concepts at your own risk.

There are many ways to express our gratitude other than saying, "Thank you." Sometimes an expression of appreciation, love, or a hug can be as effective as saying thank you. In our society there are many situations where out of courtesy we say, "Thank you." We can fall into the habit of saying, "Thank you." without really feeling it or meaning it. In most situations the receiver picks up on our insincerity and the expression is anything but gratitude.

There is a convenience store chain in our city that trains its clerks to greet each customer as they enter the store. This greeting is meant to be an expression of gratitude for the customer shopping there. For the most part it would be more effective if they had a parrot in a cage by the front door greeting the customers; however, employees in a couple of their stores have caught the spirit of gratitude and you feel their sincerity when you enter that store. If you visit that store two or three times in a week they will know your name and most likely something about you. I drive out of my way, passing two or three of their stores to get to one of those two stores.

So, the first step in gratitude exercising is to be aware of our sincerity level when we say "Thank you." For the next few days when you go out to eat, shop or any activity where you would just normally, automatically, say, "Thank you." check your sincerity level before you say it. If you feel less than sincere, stop and think about why you say, "Thank you." in that situation. What gift, value or service have you received? Think about that, then from your heart, with sincere gratitude, say, "Thank you." Do this exercise for several days and you will be surprised at how much more sincere your "Thank you." will sound even to you. And you will feel more grateful!

Then secondly, send at least one, more if you like, gratitude emails or cards each week. Think of someone who has done something special for you recently or maybe in the past that you failed to express gratitude to. It can be anything that you perceive as a gift, an act of kindness, a helping hand, or a word of encouragement. I sometimes will send an email, "Thank you for being you and for the joy you have added to my life."

The main point is to start thinking about people who have added value to your life and express gratitude to them. You might also consider giving a small gift with the "Thank you." note. You might be surprised at the response you will receive.

Years ago I was involved in a real estate deal where there were five contacts scheduled to close back to back, a domino effect. The first one had to close before the next one could close, etc. The sellers on the first contract were the buyers on the second contract and on down the line until the fifth contract closed.

Three days before the scheduled closing the loan officer handling the mortgage for the buyers on the first contract called and said, "The closing will be delayed for two weeks because someone forgot to order the appraisal."

"If the appraisal is on your desk by five p.m. tomorrow can we close on time?" I asked.

She responded, "Yes."

I then called the appraiser that I worked with. After explaining the situation he said, "One of my people will call in ten minutes to get the legal description and other information."

Ten minutes later, my phone rang and a lady asked for the legal description and said, "I was told not to touch another piece of paper until this appraisal is done."

The appraisal was at the bank before five p.m. the next day and all five closings went smoothly.

After it was all over I picked up a gift certificate and thank you card for her. Upon receiving the thank you card and gift certificate from a restaurant, tears started to flow and she said, "I have done many favors for people in the twenty years I've been in this business and this is the first time anyone has said thank you, much less given me a gift."

Try this. You might make someone's day as well as your own!

The third exercise we want to discuss is a gratitude visit. This is suggested by Dr. Robert A. Emmons in his book, *Gratitude Works*. Emmons writes about a couple who found this to be the case: "Walter and Jessica discovered this up close and personally what researchers have now learned through controlled clinical trials."

One of the most effective ways to deepen your *own* gratefulness is to write a letter of gratitude to an important person in your life whom you've never properly taken the time to thank and then visit that person to present him or her with the letter."*1 We all have people in our past who have made a major contribution to our lives and we have not let them know how much they are appreciated. In many cases we may not realize the impact they made on our lives until many years later. It may be a relative, a teacher, a minister or some saint in the church. What a special way to express gratitude.

There may be someone in that category who has passed on. Emmons indicates that there is value in writing a letter to some special person who is no longer with us and read it over for a few days reflecting on how they impacted our life. This can be a very powerful exercise in dealing with any guilt we might experience from any unfinished issues we may have with a person who has passed on.

Our fourth exercise is gratitude journaling. The following are suggestions for gratitude journaling.

1. **Should I buy a gratitude journal?** Use whatever works for you. If buying a gratitude journal would motivate you to follow through with this practice, by all means do so. I personally use a simple notebook. Some might find it more effective to just verbalize their gratitude. The important thing is to do it!

2. **When should I do my gratitude journal and how often?** Again this will vary with the individual. I do mine first thing in the morning right after my Bible study. Some might find it more effective in the evening or right before going to bed; whatever works for you. As to how often, the authorities disagree. Some say once a week, some say three times a week and others say daily. I do mine four days a week, but that is mostly due to my scheduling situation. I work at home, but three mornings a week I have to be out early in the day.

Very shortly after starting my gratitude journal I noticed that when driving I would quite often spontaneously start verbalizing gratitude. It was a shock at first, now it is normal. So do what you find to be the most effective for you.

3. **What if I don't feel grateful?** That's okay--do it anyway. Even after doing it for awhile there will be days you do not feel gratitude or feel you have no reason to be grateful. When you sincerely express gratitude several times, a shift will take place in your innermost being that will fill you with a sense of gratitude. It is a fantastic feeling of peace. Make a commitment to yourself to consistently keep a gratitude journal.

4. **How many items should I write down at a time?** Authorities disagree on this: some say three and others say five. There are days I just focus on one, then there are days I may have ten. For example, you may be feeling gratitude for your family: you have four siblings, a spouse, three children and eight grandchildren. You are grateful for each of them for different reasons. There are 16 different reasons for gratitude. The important thing is do not repeat yourself day after day.

About two weeks ago I noticed I was repeating myself. I asked myself, what do I have or enjoy that I haven't expressed gratitude for? I was drinking my morning coffee. I really enjoy my coffee first thing in the morning! I started thinking about that cup of coffee and how it came to me, it did not just appear there before me.

Many people contributed to my enjoyment of that simple pleasure. There are the people who grow the coffee beans, the people who process and package the coffee. The people who transport it, the people who unload the trucks at the warehouse. The drivers who deliver to the supermarket, the folks who stock the shelves, and the cashier who sells it to me.

That is not the end of the people who made that cup of coffee possible. You have the coffee maker, the water, the electricity, and all the people who made those elements available. I'm grateful to hundreds of people I will never meet and that is overwhelming. Just as overwhelming is the realization that I am part of something much bigger than me--that I am part of God, a universe and people that all work together to bring me a cup of coffee. I can't describe the feelings that followed that simple expression of gratitude for a simple cup of coffee.

5. **What kind of things should I write in my journal?** I divide mine into three categories. First, the easy ones; secondly, the difficult situations in my life; and thirdly, the things I believe will come to pass.

The first is thanking God for life, for grace and salvation, and for Jesus and the Holy Spirit. I also include in that category my family, friends, and any acts of kindness or gifts received. Go into detail as to why you are grateful. It's not just "Thank you God for life." etc., but what is it about life that you are grateful for? What is it about your child or your friend that you are grateful for?

Then the second category is the things that we don't like. The scripture says "In all things give thanks…." That includes the circumstances that we don't like. Nothing just happens; there is a reason for everything that God allows to come into our lives. Our gratefulness as an act of obedience aligns us with His will, allowing His purpose to be fulfilled in those circumstances.

Thirdly, express gratitude for blessings that are on their way!

One more thought before you start your gratitude exercising. What is the opposite of being grateful? It is the attitude of entitlement. The entitled says, "I deserve life. God owes me, my parents owe me, the government owes me, the company owes me, everyone owes me."

The grateful person says, "Life is a gift. All that I have, all that I am, all that I hope to have and be is a gift!"

Many of you are feeling very frustrated and thinking these are great ideas, but don't have the time to do any of these exercises. You may think you will never be able to fit this into your schedule. Many are totally covered up taking care of your family and working at a demanding career. Some of you are single parents providing for your family all by yourself while trying to get your career on track. It seems almost impossible to find any time for yourself.

There is good news though! Most of these exercises are interior work in our inner person, time that you are possibly using for negative activities such as worrying, fretting about the kids, the job, or the bills. You would give anything for a few moments of solitude. Solitude isn't always as productive as we might think. Emmons in his book, *Gratitude Works*, shares the following story that illustrates this point.

A former CEO of a major corporation, at age of fifty-nine, tires of the cutthroat rat race and desires a simpler, gentler life. He joins a monastery and takes a vow of silence in which he is allowed to say only two words every seven years.

After the first seven years, the abbot calls him in and asks if he would like to say anything.

"Bed hard." he says.

The abbot nods and whisks him away. Seven

more years pass. The abbot brings him back in and asks for his two words.

He clears his throat and says, "Food bad."

The head abbot nods and sends him away. Seven more years pass. Once again he appears before the abbot. "Do you have anything to say?" asked the abbot.

"I quit," he says.

*"That's not surprising," replied the abbot. "You've done nothing but complain ever since you got here."*2

So, we are reminded in this story that all the solitude and silence in the world doesn't guarantee emotional or spiritual growth. Yes, the Bible tells us to, "Be still, and know that I am God." (Psalm 46: 10) Yes, quiet time alone with God is essential to our spiritual growth. It is very important that we make time in our busy schedules to be alone with God in Bible study and prayer. But let's not overlook the fact that God often reveals Himself and inspires us when we are on the go.

In the scripture God spoke to many people while they were on the go. Paul was traveling on the road to Damascus when God spoke to him. God spoke to Moses from the burning bush as he was tending his father-in-law's sheep in the desert. He revealed Himself to David several times as David went about caring for his father's sheep. Jesus appeared to some of the disciples as they were walking to Emmaus. There are countless other times when God revealed Himself to people on the go. Some of my very best times with God have been when traveling in my car.

Technology offers us many possibilities. We have the Bible in audio as well as other good spiritual books. We can use our I-pad or other similar devices for gratitude journaling or sending gratitude email. The possibilities are almost limitless. Many of us have commute time that we can use to listen to God's word or other good books. We can listen as we go about the chores around the house. And don't forget self-talk. You may be surprised to learn that self-talk is going on most all the time. Let's take advantage of this and discipline ourselves to direct our self-talk to spiritual things, especially gratitude. In summing this up we challenge you with the following suggestions.

1. Always carry your gratitude journal and the Bible or a good spiritual book. Or if you prefer, carry your I-pad. You can journal, read the Bible or a book in electronic format. You never know when you will have unexpected moments of free time.

2. Become aware of your self-talk and direct it to gratitude.

3. Be alert to every moment of unexpected quiet time as you go about your chores at home.

Be creative; ask God to make you alert to the opportunities that arise throughout your very busy day. To do so will bring you many blessings and surprises.

Happy exercising! After you have done your gratitude exercises for about four weeks take the gratitude quiz again. You will be pleasantly surprised at the results!

CHAPTER THREE

Life is a Gift

"When we change the way we look at things, the things we look at change."
-Wayne Dyer

In order to develop a mindset of an attitude of gratitude many of us will need to change the way we look at life. Life is a gift from God! In fact it is a wonderful gift second only to that awesome gift of eternal life. Consider the following observations summarizing the record of creation of man in the book of Genesis by S. Michael Houdmann, *on GotQuestions.org.*

Question: "What does it mean that humanity is made in the image of God?"

Answer: On the last day of creation, God said, "Let us make man in our image, in our likeness." (Genesis 1:26). Thus, He finished His work with a "personal touch." God formed man from the dust and gave him life by sharing His own breath (Genesis 2:7). Accordingly, man is unique among all God's creations, having both a material body and an immaterial soul/spirit.

Having the "image" or "likeness" of God means, in the simplest terms, that we were made to resemble God. Adam did not resemble God in the sense of God's having flesh and blood. Scripture says that "God is spirit." (John 4:24) and therefore exists without a body. However, Adam's body did mirror the life of God insofar as it was created in perfect health and was not subject to death.

The image of God refers to the immaterial part of man. It sets man apart from the animal world, fits him for the dominion God intended him to have over the earth (Genesis 1:28), and enables him to commune with his Maker. It is a likeness--mentally, morally, and socially.

Mentally, man was created as a rational, volitional agent. In other words, man can reason and man can choose. This is a reflection of God's intellect and freedom. Anytime someone invents a machine, writes a book, paints a landscape, enjoys a symphony, calculates a sum, or names a pet, he or she is proclaiming the fact that we are made in God's image.

Morally, man was created in righteousness and perfect innocence, a reflection of God's holiness. God saw all He had made (mankind included) and called it "very good" (Genesis 1:31). Our conscience or "moral compass" is a vestige of that original state. Whenever someone writes a law, recoils from evil, praises good behavior, or feels guilty, he is confirming the fact that we are made in God's own image.

Socially, man was created for fellowship. This reflects God's triune nature and His love. In Eden, man's primary relationship was with God (Genesis 3:8 implies fellowship with God) and God made the first woman because, "It is not good for the man to be alone." (Genesis 2:18). Every time someone marries, makes a friend, hugs a child, or attends church, he is demonstrating the fact that we are made in the likeness of God.

Part of being made in God's image is that Adam had the capacity to make free choices. Although he was given a righteous nature, Adam made an evil choice to rebel against his Creator. In so doing, Adam marred the image of God within himself, and he passed that damaged likeness on to all his descendants (Romans 5:12). Today, we still bear the image of God (James 3:9), but we also bear the scars of sin. Mentally, morally, socially, and physically, we show the effects of sin.

The good news is that when God redeems an individual, He begins to restore the original image of God, creating a "new self, created to be like God in true righteousness and holiness." (Ephesians 4:24). That redemption is only available by God's grace through faith in Jesus Christ as our Savior from the sin that separates us from God (Ephesians 2:8-9). Through Christ, we are made new creations in the likeness of God (2 Corinthians 5:17).[1]

Wow! What a gift and consider all the gifts within that gift! He made man in His own likeness, not like the other creatures He created.

God created a perfect world as a gift to man. He then created perfect man and placed him in his new perfect home. God gave man rule over his home, all things that were above the earth, on the earth and beneath the earth.

God gave man a mind to think and reason so as to rule wisely over his home. He gave him an innate intelligence and a curiosity to continue to learn more.

Barnes makes the following observation of man's use of the gift of dominion over the earth. "He has made the sea his highway to the ends of the earth, the stars his pilots on the pathless ocean, the sun his bleacher and painter, the bowels of the earth the treasury from which he draws his precious and useful metals and much of his fuel, the steam his motive power, and the lightning his messenger. These are proofs of the ever growing sway of man." (Barnes Notes on Genesis 1: 26)[*2]

God gave man the gift of emotions so as to enjoy every aspect of life in his new home. He created us with passions and talents, including spiritual gifts that when used in a way that expresses our passions activates neurotransmitters and hormones in our brain that produces feelings of joy. It can be anything from witnessing the birth of a child to simply observing a beautiful sunset from a beach. Even more amazing is the fact that if we are going through a time of feeling down or depressed, we may recall a memory of a meaningful experience from the past that will release those same neurotransmitters and hormones thus producing feelings of joy. Life is a wonderful gift!

He personally knew each of us before we arrived on planet earth: "Before I formed thee in the belly I knew thee; and before thou camest forth out of the womb I sanctified thee, and I ordained thee a prophet unto the nations." (Jeramiah 1: 5) Now we know that the "prophet unto the nations" applies to Jeramiah. But each of us came into this world with a divine purpose and a set of skills, gifts and passions to fulfill that purpose. In fulfilling that purpose we experience fulfillment or as Jesus called it: abundant life. What an amazing gift and in addition to that gift we have eternal life with Him to look forward to.

For God to be consistent in creating man in His own image He had to give man a free will or the ability to make choices. The only thing man was told not to do was not to eat the fruit from a certain tree. He chose to disobey that one command. This act of disobedience brought death and chaos into this perfect world. Man was created to live forever and to walk and commune with God. But that act of disobedience brought death and separation between man and God. Note the sin here was not eating the fruit. Eating the fruit was the behavior; the sin was disobedience to God. And so it is with all sin.

But God the loving Father and creator would not see His creation destroyed. He had another plan which we see expressed in John 3:16: "For God so loved the world, that He gave His only begotten Son, that whosoever believeth in him should not perish but have everlasting life." This is the greatest gift ever given! This is God's grace freely given.

We do not deserve it nor can we earn it.

Many years ago when studying for the ministry, my uncles and grandfather said, "Roger I'm happy for you. I'm glad you can be good. I wished I could."

Being good has nothing to do with salvation. We can never be good enough. The only thing we can bring to Him is our sinfulness. Salvation is by God's grace, a free gift! The following modern parable expresses God's grace as a gift quite effectively, author unknown.

After living what I felt was a "decent" life, my time on earth came to the end. The first thing I remember is sitting on a bench in the waiting room of what I thought to be a courthouse. The doors opened and I was instructed to come in and have a seat by the defense table. As I looked around I saw the "prosecutor." He was a villainous looking gent who snarled as he stared at me. He definitely was the most evil person I have ever seen.

I sat down and looked to my left and there sat my attorney, a kind and gentle looking man whose appearance seemed so familiar to me, I felt I knew Him.

The corner door opened and there appeared the Judge in full flowing robe. He commanded an awesome presence as He moved across the room. I couldn't take my eyes off of Him. As He took His seat behind the bench, He said, "Let us begin."

The prosecutor rose and said, "My name is Satan and I am here to show you why this man belongs in hell." He proceeded to tell of lies that I told, things that I stole, and in the past when I cheated others. Satan told of other horrible perversions that were once in my life, and the more he spoke, the further down in my seat I sank. I was so embarrassed that I couldn't look at anyone, even my own attorney, as the Devil told of sins that even I had completely forgotten about.

As upset as I was at Satan for telling all these things about me, I was equally upset at my attorney who sat there silently not offering any form of defense at all. I knew I had been guilty of those things, but I had done some good in my life - couldn't that at least equal out part of the harm I'd done? Satan finished with a fury and said, "This man belongs in hell. He is guilty of all that I have charged and there is not a person who can prove otherwise."

When it was His turn, my attorney first asked if He might approach the bench. The Judge allowed this over the strong objection of Satan, and beckoned Him to come forward. As He got up and started walking, I was able to see Him in His full splendor and majesty. I realized why He seemed so familiar; this was Jesus representing me, my Lord and my Savior.

He stopped at the bench and softly said to the Judge, "HI, DAD," and then He turned to address the court.

"Satan was correct in saying that this man has sinned, I won't deny any of these allegations. And, yes, the wages of sin is death, and this man deserves to be punished."

Jesus took a deep breath and turned to His

Father with outstretched arms and proclaimed, "However, I died on the cross so that this person might have eternal life and he has accepted Me as his Savior, so he is Mine."

My Lord continued with, "His name is written in the Book of Life, and no one can snatch him from Me. Satan still does not understand yet. This man is not to be given justice, but rather mercy."

As Jesus sat down, He quietly paused, looked at His Father and said, "There is nothing else that needs to be done. I've done it all."

The Judge lifted His mighty hand and slammed the gavel down. The following words bellowed from His lips. "This man is free. The penalty for him has already been paid in full. Case dismissed."

I asked Jesus as He gave me my instructions where to go next, "Have you ever lost a case?"

Christ lovingly smiled and said, "Everyone that has come to Me and asked Me to represent them has received the same verdict as you, 'Paid In Full.'"[*3]

When we view life as a gift rather than something we deserve or are entitled to, we see many reasons to be grateful. We live this life on two planes, the human and the spiritual. Rick Warren writes in, *The Purpose Driven Life*, "When you fully comprehend that there is more to life than just here and now, and you realize that life is just preparation for eternity, you will begin to live differently. You will start living in light of eternity, and that will color how you handle every relationship, task, and circumstance. Suddenly many activities, goals, and even problems that seem so important will appear trivial, petty and unworthy of your attention. The closer you live to God, the smaller everything else appears. When you live in light of eternity your values change."*4

When we see life as a gift from God and everything that we experience as preparation for us to spend eternity with Him, we will "Give thanks in all things."

Now, the question is, how do we see life? Every event in life affects us at the spiritual level as well as the human level. Which is the most important? Whichever way we see it will determine how the things we look at appear to us. If we see the most important effects of every event that occurs in our life to be of a spiritual nature and we realize in everything that happens God is equipping us to fulfill our purpose and spend eternity with Him, then we find reason to, "Give thanks in all things."

CHAPTER FOUR

When we are in an Attitude of Gratitude we are...

1. Acting in obedience to God.
2. Rejoicing.
3. Praying.
4. Acting in faith and trust.

"Rejoice evermore. Pray without ceasing. In everything give thanks; for this is the will of God in Christ Jesus concerning you." (1Thessalonians 5: 16-18) Several Bible scholars believe that the phrase, "For this is God's will for you in Christ Jesus," applies to verse 16 and 17 as well as verse 18. There is no doubt that it applies to, "Give thanks in all things." It most likely applies to "Rejoice evermore," and "Pray without ceasing." because gratitude is a form of rejoicing and prayer. The fact that this phrase is used here gives gratitude a very high priority in the Christian's life. When the phrase, "For this is God's will for you" is used other places in scripture it refers to belief in Jesus Christ as our Lord and Savior.

Acting in Obedience to God

"For this is the will of God - That ye should be always happy; that ye should ever be in the spirit of prayer; and that ye should profit by every occurrence in life, and be continually grateful and obedient; for gratitude and obedience are inseparably connected." Adam Clark.[1]

It was disobedience that caused the fall of man. The sin was not eating the forbidden fruit, that was the behavior. The sin was disobedience. That disobedience caused a separation between God and man, between man and his real self and between man and man. Obedience to God reconnects us; we become one with God, with ourselves and with our fellow man.

Obedience and disobedience is a strange creature, it is sometimes rebellion, but more often it is simply an innocent curiosity. This is what makes it so dangerous; this was true in Eve's case. This is a tool the tempter uses often. He is very subtle. He can sneak up on us before we realize what's happening. Eve was curious as to what was different about the fruit from the forbidden tree. The fact that it was forbidden made it appear to be special.

I remember the first time I consciously decided to disobey. I was three years old. My grandmother and aunt took me shopping with them in a department store in Louisville, Ky. This was my first time in a city that I remember. In those days they had segregated water fountains and bathrooms. They showed me the water fountains and the toilet; one labeled for whites, the other for colored. They told me to use the one labeled white and not to use the one labeled colored.

That seemed very strange. What was so special about the one labeled colored that I couldn't use them? That water fountain must be filled with Orange Nehi or RC Cola. And what was in those toilets? Indoor plumbing was a mystery to me anyway. Well, I was determined to find out.

Yeah, you got it. Disappointment, nothing but water in that water fountain. I never did make it to the toilet, got caught every time I tried. But I'm sure there were no Sears and Roebuck or Montgomery Ward catalogs and probably no corn cobs. Hey, there's something to be grateful for, TP. How like our spiritual life, disobedience to God always brings disappointment.

Obedience has a negative connotation for most of us. It quite often involved doing something we didn't want to do. It meant to follow the orders of the teacher, our parents or some other adult. As we grew up (which took a lot longer for some of us) we developed feelings of love, affection, admiration and trust for our parents and other adult figures in our life, thus creating situations that we wanted to obey.

When we realize the tremendous gift of life and eternal life God has given us, we want to obey Him out of gratitude! "A sense of Gratitude is not the same as a feeling of indebtedness. Indebtedness causes a feeling that one must repay a benefactor. Gratitude causes one to reach out to their benefactor to improve their relationship with them."[*2] We see this in Zacchaeus in the gospel of Luke.

I want use the words of Tullian Tchividjian in telling the Zacchaeus story. He tells it so graphically in his book, *One Way Love,* that you can almost see and hear the wee little man.

"As the chief tax collector, the Jewish establishment would have despised him because he collected taxes for Rome, an act that was considered both traitorous and sinful. Yet as a Jew, he would have been shunned by his imperial employers as well. Even the other tax collectors would have hated him, because he likely cheated them, too, skimming funds off of the top of their ill-gotten cash. Add to the mix an inevitable Napoleon complex, and you have a picture of a loathsome loan shark who used his authority to extort his countrymen for both personal gain and that of the occupying Roman government.

"[Jesus] entered Jericho and was passing through.

"And behold, there was a man named Zacchaeus. He was a chief tax collector and was rich.

"And he was seeking to see who Jesus was, but on account of the crowd he could not, because he was small in stature.

"So he ran on ahead and climbed up into a sycamore tree to see him, for he was about to pass that way.

"And Jesus came to the place , he looked up and said to him, 'Zacchaeus, hurry and come down, for I must stay at your house today.'

"So he hurried and came down and received him joyfully. (Luke 19: 1-6)

"Jesus singled out Zacchaeus, despite the fact that Zacchaeus had not said or done anything to warrant or attract his attention. Zacchaeus simply did what he would for any passing sideshow, namely, climb a tree , so he could catch a glimpse of what was going on. There was no gesture of repentance, no prayers, no tears, no words! The initiative belonged to Jesus alone. And Jesus didn't say, 'I want to stay at your house,' or 'Would you be so kind as to invite me over for tea?' He said, 'I must stay at your house.' The request is less of a request than an imperative.

"The Response:

"We can safely assume that Zacchaeus would be taken aback that Jesus wanted to spend time with him. You can almost hear his incredulous reply, 'You want to come to my house? You want to associate with me? Are you sure you got the right guy?' That's conjecture, of course, but the broad strokes of his response in the text are remarkable. 'So [Zacchaeus] hurried and came down and received him joyfully.' Zacchaeus did not hesitate to respond to Jesus.—there was no scoffing, no song and dance, just enthusiasm and joy. Christ's entreaty inspires!

"We might wonder how long it had been since anyone other than fellow tax collectors and perhaps a few lowlife friends had visited Zacchaeus. Did he actually have any friends or family? He would have had to work hard to become the chief tax collector: he probably would have had to sacrifice more than a few relationships on the altar of ambition. Maybe he had tried to satisfy himself with the luxury and self-indulgence that his riches afforded him, and maybe he had found that rather than satiating his appetite, they only made it worse. Maybe he was both lonely and desperate. Whatever the case, the immediacy and exuberance of his response suggests that no one had to tell Zacchaeus he was lost. He was all too aware of his station.

"What happened next is even more shocking. 'And Zacchaeus stood and said to the Lord, Behold, Lord, the half of my goods I give to the poor. And if I have defrauded anyone of anything, I restore it fourfold.' (Luke 19: 8).

"The fruit of grace in this instance was spontaneous, borderline absurd generosity. This is what the apostle John meant when he wrote, 'We love because he first loved us.' (1 John 4:19). He inverts the way we normally think about these things. Jesus approached Zacchaeus before he had a chance to exhibit any receptiveness, let alone sorrow or eagerness. What's more, at no point did Jesus lean in and tell his new friend, 'Listen, I don't want to embarrass you in front of everyone, but you and I both know you need to clean up your act. If you want to continue hanging out, you need to make things right, starting with your pocketbook.' Zacchaeus's joyful charity was not the preface to God's grace—it was its result.

"The truth is, Jesus didn't require anything of

Zacchaeus. He didn't force, coerce, or guilt Zacchaeus into giving back what he stole; he just loved him. And yet the natural fruit—and what is fruit if not natural?—of this one way love turned out to be far more extravagant then anything Christ would have suggested. Obedience would be too weak a word to describe Zacchaeus actions. Nowhere in the law does it require a person to give half of their goods to the poor. Similarly, repaying someone you have defrauded by a factor of four is far beyond the call of duty. Zacchaeus does more than the right thing, and he does it spontaneously, cheerfully, and abundantly.

"A grateful heart is a generous heart, and a generous heart is a liberated heart. It is no coincidence that the very thing to which Zacchaeus was most enslaved – money is the very thing he was inspired to give away so freely.

"This isn't just how things work in the Bible—this is real life. Gratitude is the starting point. Zacchaeus was so overwhelmed by gratitude for the love and acceptance he experienced from Jesus that it caused him to go beyond obedience." [3]

All of us have had a similar response when we first experience God's grace in our lives. But it is so easy to slip back into legalism if we don't stay focused on Jesus and be constantly reminded of His love and grace. A very short time after my life was totally transformed by God's grace, my wife, who is an RN, was asked to participate in a free clinic giving the polio vaccine and other shots to underprivileged families on a Sunday.

I said, "No, not on Sunday." I soon realized

that I was being just as legalistic as the Pharisees who criticized Jesus for healing on the Sabbath. May we stay focused on Jesus so that an awareness of His love and grace is constant, producing a mindset of an attitude of gratitude!

Rejoicing: "Rejoice Evermore."

An attitude of gratitude will produce feelings of joy! To rejoice is an expression of joy. The apostle Paul set a very high standard for us in regards to gratitude, joy, praise and prayer. It was to keep Jesus first and foremost in all circumstances in our lives. But Paul held himself to that same standard or perhaps an even higher standard. We see this in Acts 16: 20-34.

20 And brought them to the magistrates, saying, these men, being Jews, do exceedingly trouble our city,

21 And teach customs, which are not lawful for us to receive, neither to observe, being Romans.

22 And the multitude rose up together against them: and the magistrates rent off their clothes, and commanded to beat them.

23 And when they had laid many stripes upon them, they cast them into prison, charging the jailor to keep them safely:

24 Who, having received such a charge, thrust them into the inner prison, and made their feet fast in the stocks.

25 And at midnight Paul and Silas prayed, and sang praises unto God: and the prisoners heard them.

26 And suddenly there was a great earthquake, so that the foundations of the prison were shaken: and immediately all the doors were opened, and every one's bands were loosed.

27 And the keeper of the prison awaking out of his sleep, and seeing the prison doors open, he drew out his sword, and would have killed himself, supposing that the prisoners had been fled.

28 But Paul cried with a loud voice, saying, Do thyself no harm: for we are all here.

29 Then he called for a light, and sprang in, and came trembling, and fell down before Paul and Silas,

30 And brought them out, and said, Sirs, what must I do to be saved?

31 And they said, Believe on the Lord Jesus Christ, and thou shalt be saved, and thy house.

32 And they spake unto him the word of the Lord, and to all that were in his house.

33 And he took them the same hour of the night, and washed their stripes; and was baptized, he and all his, straightway.

34 And when he had brought them into his house, he set meat before them, and rejoiced, believing in God with all his house.

Wow, can you imagine what that would be like, to be beaten within an inch of your life, put in stocks in the inner most part of a dark, dingy prison with other real criminals just for sharing the gospel of Jesus Christ? Paul was not a robust, healthy man He probably didn't get adequate sleep nor eat a healthy diet. And now his back was nothing but a slab of raw meat. It would have been easy to become depressed and full of self-pity, but not Paul. He said, "I think it is time for a prayer meeting. We will rejoice, praise God and pray."

That was an attitude of gratitude that moved him into the flow of God's blessings. Look what happened: there was an earthquake that freed the prisoners. He didn't flee when he had the opportunity because God was not finished. There was more to do, the conversion of the jailer and his household. And notice what happened next. The jailer brought them into his home and the prayer meeting continued. Paul set an example here for rejoicing and praising God in all situations that will produce joy and the fulfillment of God's will in our lives!

Praying: "Pray Without Ceasing."

Have you ever wondered how that was possible? If we pray all the time how do we ever get anything else done? How can I go around on my knees 24 hours a day, seven days a week? When do I work, sleep, spend time with family or friends, attend church or have any recreation time? I can't drive my car on my knees with my eyes closed. There is good news, when we are in an attitude of gratitude we are in fact praying! There are several different kinds of prayer. There is gratitude prayer, prayers of petition, intercessory prayer and praying in the Spirit.

In doing our gratitude exercises we offer a prayer of gratitude to God for a particular gift and/or person. In focusing on that situation or person we quite often find ourselves moving to a prayer of petition or intercessory prayer. Just this morning I was expressing gratitude for my daughter and our phone conservation yesterday. She is going through a relocation process. A new job, new house, and new schools, one of the most stressful experiences we have in everyday life. So I just naturally moved from a prayer of gratitude to a prayer of petition asking God to protect and give wisdom in all the decisions and logistics involved in her relocation process.

Gratitude connects us with God. Prayer is talking with God. When we are grateful we are communicating with God, therefore we are praying. So when we develop the mindset of an attitude of gratitude we are praying without ceasing!

Acting in Faith and Trust

"Trust in the LORD with all thine heart; and lean not unto thine own understanding." (Prov. 3:5) There is a difference between faith and trust in God.

Developing a mindset of an attitude of gratitude requires a firm unshakable trust in God. It is more than a belief in the existence of God. The scriptures say, "Thou believest that there is one God; thou doest well: the devils also believe, and tremble." (James 2:19)

Trust is total abandonment to the Divine mind, which carries us beyond our own intelligences, abilities and circumstances. Yes, we are saved by faith, belief in Jesus Christ and His grace provided for us by His life, death, resurrection and ascension to heaven where He intercedes for us. But to grow into a mature Christian, that faith must become a strong unmovable trust in God. A trust that causes us to believe in His unconditional love; to believe that He wants the very best for us; that He knows what is the very best and is capable of bringing it to pass.

This kind of trust is possible only by truly knowing the one in whom we trust. We can know Him in that way only by spending time with Him. It is more than knowing about Him. Growing this trust requires spending time in His presence in prayer, praise, worship and in His word.

In the first four years of my pastoral experience, in 1966, we built two church buildings. "We" being the members of the congregation and myself. We hired skilled tradesmen and the congregation provided the labor. I was the chief laborer, when no one else could be there I was the chosen one.

For eighteen months of my first four years pastoring I was working on the church building forty plus hours per week instead of working at building the "church." Saturday was the day most of the congregation was available and the tradesmen had agreed to work on Saturdays. So I felt I should be there too. In addition to working on the church building I conducted three services per week, made a minimum of twenty-five pastoral visits per week plus overseeing the programs of the church and I had a wife and three children. Was I effective at any of my responsibilities? If so, it was only by the grace of God.

The time I had to spend with God, getting to really know Him was around midnight when I could hardly keep my eyes open. The reality is that the sheep were not fed well, my family life suffered and I was sleepwalking a good share of the time. Is this a self-pity party? No, you see I thought I was doing God's will. But I was "doing ministry."

Is it any wonder that my children grew up thinking I was too busy for them. They thought they had to go to their mother and have her make an appointment for them to spend time with me.

A few years later when facing a real crisis, I failed because I had not learned to totally trust God. Oh, I believed that He existed and that He could do all things. But I didn't trust His unconditional love; that He wanted the best for me; that He had my back. I hadn't spent time with Jesus to get to really know Him well enough to totally trust Him. In short I hadn't totally fallen in love with Him.

I heard a story many years ago that describes the difference between faith and trust. The author of this story is unknown or as one person said, "known only by God." There was this tightrope walker who was performing at Niagara Falls. He walked the tightrope across the falls entertaining a large crowd. He then pushed a wheel barrel across on the tightrope. The crowd went wild with enthusiasm.

He turned to the crowd and asked if they believed he could push the wheel barrel across with a man in it.

Many responded with an enthusiastic yes.

Then he asked for someone to get into the

wheel barrel. No one responded to that request.*4

It is one thing to believe but another thing to truly trust; to get into the wheel barrel. If I had trusted God during that crisis I would have gotten into the wheel barrel. That is, I would have been grateful knowing that His will would be worked out and that it would be the very best for me.

Allow me to play the role of prophet for a moment. All this happened during the "Jesus Movement," from the mid 60's through the early 70's. It was a great time of revival across this country with thousands of young people coming to Jesus. I can't describe how exciting and wonderful this was. But during that time there was a strong emphasis on, "doing ministry" and institutionalizing the new converts with little emphasis on discipleship.

There was too much concern about making them Baptist, Methodist, Assembly of God, Nazarene or Catholic, etc. Yes, there were Catholics as part of that awakening. There was a charismatic movement within the Catholic Church with many priests involved across the country. We were so busy "doing ministry" for Jesus and teaching new converts the dogma of the denomination we represented that there was little if any time left for discipling.

I can't but wonder what the visible church would look like today if we the leaders had spent more time with Jesus and minister with Him instead of for Him. There certainly would have been more discipling happening. The visible church, in general (there are some exceptions) failed to benefit from a tremendous opportunity of growth and power. Only God knows about the invisible church.

There is no way this next point can be overstated. We are about to experience another revival in this country. There is a spiritual stirring starting at the grass roots. People at the grass roots are getting fed up with the ungodliness that has taken our country by storm the last few years. People are restless, starting to ask tough questions. There is a lot more prayer going up than many of us realize.

In times like these God reveals Himself. Church, get prepared, they are coming your way-- new converts. May we be prepared to disciple. May we be able to look back a generation from now, if Jesus tarries, and see a church that is vibrant and a mighty influence on its society. We must spend time with Jesus in Bible study and prayer. We must know Him instead of just knowing about Him. Let's fall totally and madly in love with Him until we trust Him without question, beyond a shadow of any doubt whatsoever. Then and only then are we ready to make disciples from new converts. Gratitude is a big part of discipleship. May we develop a mindset of an attitude of gratitude that we can pass along to new converts!

Note: It requires some trust in God to be grateful, but as we practice gratitude our trust will grow. Whatever your trust level allows you to be grateful for, start there and experience your trust and gratitude levels growing, feeding one on the other.

CHAPTER FIVE

The Benefits of an Attitude of Gratitude

Many of us often think of God as an old man with a stern, stoic fixed expression on His face, covered with a long flowing white beard. We think of Him as the one who created the universe. The next morning He was bored, so, He said, "I think I will make a creature kind of like me and give him a test." He created man, gave him the Ten Commandments, the Beatitudes and many other rules, and said, "Let's see if he can pass this test." That would be cruel and that is not a true picture of God and creation, even though some of us think of Him that way at times by default.

He created us out of love and compassion to have fellowship and communion with Him. Yes, He gave us rules to live by, but those rules were given out of love for us. As our creator, He knows us far better than we can know ourselves. He knows what will give us a sense of fulfillment in this life and prepare us to spend eternity with Him. In living by His rules we fulfill our purpose. So it is no surprise that there are many benefits from having an attitude of gratitude.

I have been fascinated by the subject of gratitude as expressed in 1 Thessalonians. (5:18) for close to forty years. It has been just the last three years that I have gotten serious about it. It has become almost an obsession. I started gratitude journaling three years ago and the results are amazing! Thank you, God! When I started research for this book about 18 months ago, I was amazed to find that there was a new movement in the field of psychology, started in the year 2000 called, "positive psychology."

Psychology departments in universities across the country began doing scientific studies on the effect of gratitude on our lives. Dr. Robert A. Emmons of the University of California, Davis, was the pioneer and leader in this work. They have studied hundreds of people from the age of eight to eighty and the results have been amazing. (Information can be found in the notes at end of this book where you can look up these studies.) People who had focused on developing gratitude for a short period of time by gratitude journaling and other gratitude exercises experienced profound results. They showed improvement in their general health, mental health, relationships and became more spiritual minded.

Many showed signs of stronger immune systems, less aches and pains, less symptoms of illness and greater flexibility. Many said they were sleeping better than they had for years and feeling more rested. This could account for some of the other changes. Some reported starting to exercise and in general made a commitment to take better care of their bodies. It seems that when we practice gratitude we become aware that life is a gift and develop a desire to take better care of ourselves. Along with this, there were reports of lower blood pressure.

I experienced the lower blood pressure and have discontinued my medication after consulting with my doctor; however, I monitor it daily. In my case the lower blood pressure was most likely due to losing thirty pounds within a six month period. I became more aware that what we eat affects our overall health. After considering several options I decided that vegetarian was the way for me to go. You don't have to count calories or weigh your food or even spend a lot of time reading labels. It's easy and it works for me.

Many of the people in the studies were able to deal with stress more effectively. Those who were challenged by depression learned ways of dealing with their depression more effectively. There was an increase in self-esteem.

Many experienced an improvement in their relationships at home, at school and in the work place. That one is fairly easy to understand; grateful people are much more fun to be around than negative, complaining, hateful people!

This reminds me of an experience I had back in the 70's, a long time before I became aware of the importance of an attitude of gratitude. A friend who owned a real estate company called and talked about the hostile environment in his office. He had about twenty people on staff. The hostility level was so high that he didn't even want to go into the office and it seemed that a lot of the employees were feeling the same way.

He asked if I would be willing to spend an evening with them and get them straightened out. Without thinking, I said yes. (A situation "Where fools rush in where angels fear to tread.") I had done some sales training for his company and was familiar with most of his people. This was Monday. We decided to have this special sales meeting on that Thursday evening.

So, now what am I going to do? I had little time to prepare with a busy schedule between Monday and Thursday. And I wasn't sure what to do anyway. Talk about being on a hot seat. But the results exceeded our expectations!

I started out with a little warmup talk about teamwork and how we are all in this together. Then I next divided them into groups of two for some interaction. They were instructed to tell the other person something that they appreciated about them. If nothing came to mind, look at what the person was wearing; it could be as simple as "I like your tie."

Then they were to think of something that person had done in the workplace that they appreciated. This all sounds very simple, but the results were amazing. Before the evening was over there were many tears shed as people confessed resentments and asked forgiveness. It was like a revival meeting. This was a small community and some of these folks had a long history. Some of them had even gone to high school together. Some of their resentments went back to high school.

What happened here? I wasn't even aware of it at the time, but what happened was gratitude! To appreciate someone or something is a form of gratitude. When we express gratitude we begin to feel it. Gratitude reproduces in like kind. It is contagious! The place they had been avoiding, they now did not want to leave. That meeting went two hours beyond the scheduled time. I saw similar results in several companies after that. Gratitude is powerful: it will change our lives.

Allow me to digress just a moment before we get into the spiritual benefits of gratitude. We want to mention some myths about gratitude. Dr. Emmons says there are five:

Five Myths about Gratitude

For more than a decade, I have devoted my career to the study of gratitude. My research, and research by my colleagues, has linked gratitude to a host of psychological, physical, and social benefits: stronger immune systems, lower blood pressure, more feelings of joy, and a greater sense of social connection, among many others.

Even armed with years of scientific data, making the case for gratitude can still be an uphill battle. At times I've been confronted with objections, reservations, or flat out hostility to the idea that gratitude is a virtue, or that we should devote more energy to cultivating an attitude of gratitude.

While I appreciate the questions and concerns people have about gratitude, I think many of the objections are based on fundamental myths or misconceptions about what gratitude really is. And unfortunately, these misconceptions deter people from practicing gratitude—and reaping its many rewards.

Here's my take on five of the most pervasive myths about gratitude.

1. Gratitude leads to complacency.

I've often heard the claim that if you're grateful, you're not going to be motivated to challenge the status quo or improve your lot in life. You'll just be satisfied, complacent, lazy and lethargic, perhaps passively resigned to an injustice or bad situation. You'll give up trying to change something.

In fact, studies suggest that the opposite is true: Gratitude not only doesn't lead to complacency, it drives a sense of purpose and a desire to do more.

My colleagues and I have found that people are actually more successful at reaching their goals when they consciously practice gratitude. When we ask people to identify six personal goals on which they want to work over the next 10 weeks—these could be academic, spiritual, social, or health-related goals, like losing weight—we find that study participants randomly assigned to keep a gratitude journal, recording five things for which they're grateful once a week, exert more effort toward those goals than participants who aren't made to practice gratitude. In fact, the grateful group makes 20 percent more progress toward their goals than the non-grateful group—but they don't stop there. They report still continuing to strive harder toward their goals.

This finding does not surprise me because people made to keep a gratitude journal in my studies consistently report feeling more energetic, alive, awake, and alert. Yet they don't report feeling more satisfied with their progress toward their goals than other people do. They don't become complacent or satisfied to the point that they stop making an effort.

This relates to other research showing that gratitude inspires "pro-social" behavior such as generosity, compassion, and charitable giving— none of which suggests passivity or resignation. Instead, it suggests that gratitude motivates people to go out and do things for others—to give back, I think, some of the goodness that they recognize receiving themselves.

In fact, my colleagues and I published a study in Motivation and Emotion a few years ago which found that kids who were more grateful than their peers at age 10 were by age 14 performing more pro-social activities and feeling greater social integration, meaning that they wanted to give back to their community and family. Again, the grateful people didn't show passive resignation; they were out in the world doing stuff to make life better for others.

All this evidence supports an observation made

by William Damon, the noted developmental psychologist, in his book *The Path to Purpose*, which is about how we can help kids find their calling in life. "The sense of gratitude for being able to partake in what the world has to offer, and to have a chance to make one's own contribution," writes Damon, "is common in those with a sense of purpose."

2. Gratitude is just a naïve form of positive thinking.

Some people claim that gratitude is just about thinking nice thoughts and expecting good things—and ignores the negativity, pain, and suffering in life.

Well, evidence shows it's much more than that. Based on my research, I've come to define gratitude as a specific way of thinking about receiving a benefit and giving credit to others besides oneself for that benefit. In fact, gratitude can be very difficult because it requires that you recognize your dependence on others, and that's not always positive. You have to humble yourself, in the sense that you have to become a good receiver of others' support and generosity. That can be very hard—most people are better givers than receivers.

What's more, feelings of gratitude can sometimes stir up related feelings of indebtedness and obligation, which doesn't sound like positive thinking at all. If I am grateful for something you provided to me, I have to take care of that thing—I might even have to reciprocate at some appropriate time in the future. That type of indebtedness or obligation can be perceived very negatively—it can cause people real discomfort.

The data bear this out: When people are grateful, they aren't necessarily free of negative emotions—we don't find that they necessarily have less anxiety or less tension or less unhappiness. Practicing gratitude magnifies positive feelings more than it reduces negative feelings. If it was just positive thinking, or just a form of denial, you'd experience no negative thoughts or feelings when you're keeping a gratitude journal, for instance. But, in fact, people do.

So gratitude isn't just a nice, warm, fuzzy feeling. It has responsibilities that go along with it that can make it difficult or challenging for people under certain circumstances.

3. Gratitude makes us too self-effacing.

Some people assume that if I am grateful, I give credit to others for my own success. When I recognize the ways others have helped me, I risk overlooking my own hard work or natural abilities.

Research suggests that's not the case. In one study, researchers administered a purportedly difficult test and told the study participants that they could win money for doing well on the test. Then the participants received a helpful hint that would help them get a high score.

All the participants regarded the hint as helpful. But only those who felt personally responsible for their own score felt grateful for the hint. Gratitude was actually associated with a greater sense of personal control over one's success.

We have corroborated this in other studies: Grateful people give credit to others, but not at the expense of acknowledging their own responsibility for their success. They take credit, too. It's not either/or—either I did this all myself or somebody else did it for me. Instead, they recognize their own feats and abilities while also feeling gratitude toward the people—parents, teachers—who helped them along the way.

4. Gratitude isn't possible—or appropriate—in the midst of adversity or suffering.

Some argue that it's impossible to be grateful in the midst of suffering. When life is going well, when there's abundance—sure, then we can be grateful. But what about when we're facing hard times?

I believe not only is gratitude possible in those circumstances—it's vital to helping us get through them. When faced with adversity, gratitude helps us see the big picture and not feel overwhelmed by the setbacks we're facing in the moment. And as I've suggested above, that attitude of gratitude can actually motivate us to tackle the challenges before us. Without a doubt, it can be hard to take this grateful perspective, but research suggests it is possible, and it is worth it.

Consider a study led by my colleague Philip Watkins, published in the Journal of Positive Psychology, in which participants were asked to recall an unpleasant, unresolved memory—a time they were victimized or betrayed or hurt in some way that still made them upset. The participants were randomly assigned to complete one of three different writing exercises, one of which involved focusing on positive aspects of the upsetting experience and considering how it might now make them feel grateful.

The results showed that the gratitude group reported feeling more closure and less unpleasant emotions than participants who didn't write about their experience from a grateful perspective. The grateful writers weren't told to deny or ignore the negative aspects of their memory. Yet they seemed more resilient in the face of those troubles.

Similarly, roughly a decade ago, I asked people suffering from severe neuromuscular disorders to keep a gratitude journal over two weeks. Given that much of their lives involved intense discomfort and visits to pain clinics, I wondered whether they'd be able to find anything to be grateful for. Yet not only did they find reasons to be grateful, but they also experienced significantly more positive emotions than a similar group that didn't keep a gratitude journal. The gratitude group also felt more optimistic about the upcoming week, felt more connected to others (even though many of them lived alone) and reported getting more sleep each night—an important indicator of overall health and well-being.

So again, this is a gratitude myth that can be debunked. Science suggests we can cultivate or maintain an attitude of gratitude through hard times, and that we'll be better for it.

5. You have to be religious to be grateful.

This myth is easy to bust: The new science of gratitude has clearly shown that people can have a grateful disposition even if they're not religious. What's more, it's possible to boost levels of gratitude in people regardless of whether they're religious. While some research suggests that religious people might be more inclined to feel or practice gratitude, they are by no means the only ones who score high on gratitude scales.

And among religious people, feeling grateful to God isn't mutually exclusive with feeling grateful to other potential sources of goodness. In some of my research, we've asked people to identify the sources of their success and positive qualities, like their intelligence or attractiveness. People who score high in gratitude are more likely to give credit to God than are people who score low in gratitude. But those grateful people are more likely to give credit across the board, meaning that they also give credit to other sources, such as other people, genetics, and hard work.

I believe many of these myths spring from a fundamental misconception about gratitude; that it is a simplistic emotion. But part of what has kept me interested in gratitude for roughly 15 years is that it is deceptively complicated; each year I seem to encounter another nuance or layer to it. Once we appreciate these complexities of gratitude, documented by years of scientific research, we are in a better position to enjoy all the strengths and goodness it can bring.[1]

We place these myths about gratitude in this chapter on the benefits of gratitude because the response to each of these myths indicates other benefits of gratitude.

The studies also showed spiritual growth; many reported becoming more spiritual minded. In the next few paragraphs I want to show some spiritual benefits from scripture and from my own experience and observation. When we have an attitude of gratitude we experience many benefits. 1. We become inspired by God. 2. We are more aware of Him and hear His voice more clearly. 3. His will for our life becomes clearer to us. 4. We are able to detach more easily or as it has been said, we "Let go and let God." 5. We move into the flow of His blessings.

Inspiration

When we are in an attitude of gratitude to the point that we experience a shift in our innermost being, we may experience divine inspiration. There are many synonyms for inspire. The one that applies to divine inspiration is inspirit. Inspirit means "To infuse spirit or life into: to enliven." It is the spirit of God within us.

The Old Testament often proclaims the phrase, "The spirit of the Lord came upon him." When this happened, the person whom the spirit came upon was infused with supernatural power, enabling him to see or perceive something he couldn't see with the natural eye; or to perform an act that was beyond the capability of natural man. Such was the case with Samson (Judges 15:14.) "And when he came unto Lehi, the Philistines shouted against him; and the Spirit of the Lord came mightily upon him, and the cords that were upon his arms became as flax that was burnt with fire, and his bands loosed from off his hands."

Jesus said, "Verily, verily, I say unto you, he that believeth on me, the works that I do shall he do also; and greater works than these shall he do; because I go unto my Father." (John 14:12) Jesus had promised that when He returned to the Father He would send the Holy Spirit, the comforter, the great enabler. Through Him and by Him we would be empowered to do these great things.

"And when the day of Pentecost was fully come, they were all with one accord in one place. And suddenly there came a sound from heaven as of a rushing mighty wind, and it filled all the house where they were sitting. And there appeared unto them cloven tongues like as of fire, and it sat upon each of them. And they were all filled with the Holy Ghost, and began to speak with other tongues, as the Spirit gave them utterance." (Acts 2: 1-4)

"But the manifestation of the Spirit is given to every man to profit withal. For to one is given by the Spirit the word of wisdom; to another the word of knowledge by the same Spirit; to another faith by the same Spirit; to another the gifts of healing by the same Spirit; to another the working of miracles; to another prophecy; to another discerning of spirits; to another diverse kinds of tongues; to another the interpretation of tongues: But all these worketh that one and the selfsame Spirit, dividing to every man severally as he will." (1 Corinthians 12: 7-11)

That same Holy Spirit is still active today inspiring and enabling us to preform way beyond our natural capabilities. In difficult and confusing times, He infuses us with divine wisdom enabling us to make wise decisions. When dealing with challenges, He enlightens us with divine knowledge. He performs miracles in and through us. He enables us to love and forgive when the human part of us wants revenge.

Yes, an attitude of gratitude will often bring us divine inspiration. Inspiration makes us a lot bigger, stronger, more intelligent, wiser, and more loving than we are capable of being in our natural self.

Increases our God Consciousness

Developing a mindset of an attitude of gratitude will increase our awareness of God. It enables us to hear, recognize and respond to the voice of God. "My sheep hear my voice, and I know them, and they follow me." (John 27: 27)

Yes, God still speaks to us today, but His voice is often obscured due to all the other voices demanding our attention. We have thousands of voices calling to us every minute via stimuli received by our five senses. Often some place in all this noise is the voice of God. But we can know His voice, as our awareness of Him grows by practicing gratitude in all things.

God speaks to us through His word, through other people, through circumstances and through His voice. Let me hasten to say, God's voice will always be consistent with His nature and His written word. Whenever someone commits a violent evil act and says, "God told me to do it," they are very mistaken. It was most likely the voice of an evil spirit or a symptom of a mental disorder.

He speaks to most of us through His written word. This is why it is so important for us to be in His word daily, that we might know Him better and mature in our daily life. He also speaks to us through others, such as pastors, teachers and fellow believers. This is why church worship and Bible study groups are important to our growth.

God also speaks to us through dreams, visions and a voice. Again, if it is His voice, the message will be consistent with His nature and written word.

In almost every negative event in my life I was warned ahead of time by a small still voice. About ten years ago I had this habit of unlocking my office door, then instead of putting my keys back into my pocket I would lay them on a book shelf to the left of my desk. One day as I threw my keys on the shelf a small, still voice said, "You better put them in your pocket." I ignored it.

About two o'clock I was getting ready to go to lunch, guess what, my keys were not there. So I went around to the back parking lot. My car was gone. It had been stolen. I have had similar experiences more times than I can remember. Then there are the times I heeded the voice; therefore, I'm not sure of what kind of event God protected me from. Many of you probably have experienced a time when you were in route to a certain location and had your route planned.

Then suddenly there was a small voice or inner prompting that said, "Go a different way." I'm convinced that is God protecting us from delays or accidents. A couple of times I learned afterwards, via the news, that the decision to take a different route saved me from long traffic delays due to accidents.

God sometimes communicates a message through a combination of methods. One weekend back in the 70's my wife had taken the children to visit the grandparents. Saturday evening I was at my office until about ten P.M. I went home, went to bed, had just dozed off and I heard this voice calling my name. I thought it was a dream. I started to go back to sleep and there was the voice.

This time I knew it was not a dream. I wasn't asleep. So I said, "What?" Then came an impression from deep inside: "George."

George was my next door neighbor. He had a drinking problem and was going through a divorce he didn't want. It was a difficult time in George's life.

I went next door, all the lights were on, the front door open, but no George. There was a full moon, as I walked around to the back of the house I saw him as clear as day. He was standing about hundred yards away from the house with a shot gun.

He was trying to put the barrel of the gun into his mouth. After an hour I got the gun from him. It was a long night. George got his act together and lived a very productive life ministering to others with similar problems.

Yes, God speaks today to guide us, protect us and mature us. But we must hear and heed His message. His messages of warnings are sometimes to help us to avoid a negative, difficult or painful experience. But sometimes these experiences can't be avoided. His message is to prepare us to handle them in a way that is pleasing to Him.

In the early 70's I had this recurring dream over a period of two years. It was a depressing dream. I spent some time in trying to learn the meaning of the dream, but not the time that I should have. I was back and forth with the idea that, "This is God trying to tell me something" to, "This is just a dream that has no meaning." A couple years later I realized that the dream was God's warning about a coming event in my life that I needed to prepare for.

Relating to that same situation God warned me through another person, my father, but I failed to hear it. In May of 1972 I had a meeting to attend at Olivet Nazarene College in Bourbonnais, Illinois. My parents lived sixty miles from Olivet. They drove up for dinner my last evening there and I thank God for that evening.

That was the last time I saw my dad, he died about three weeks later. But I wish to this day that I had listened to what God was saying to me through my dad that evening. Dad got in his car to leave, then he pulled over, got out of his car and came back to where I was and said, "Roger, your mother and I are very proud of you and what you are doing with your life. But your most important responsibility is your kids at home. Don't ever forget that and consider that maybe you are spending too much time away from them."

If I had only listened, it would not have changed the event, but I would have been prepared to deal with it within God's will. It was the most devastating event in my live and it almost destroyed me. If I had recognized God's voice and prepared by spending more time in His word and totally trusting in Jesus, many years of my life would have been different and more productive for His kingdom. But thank God for His love and grace!

When we develop a mindset of an attitude of gratitude we become more aware of God in our lives. The consciousness of His presence enables us to hear and respond to His voice.

Manifest the Will of God

An attitude of gratitude enables us to manifest the will of God more definitely in our lives. Much of God's will for us is revealed in His written word. For example, we know from His word that it is His will for all to come to Christ in faith and repentance and receive Him as our Lord and savior. We know that we are to, "Walk in the light as He is in the light." (John 1:7) We know we are to live a holy life. We know it is His will for us to meet together with fellow believers "Not forsaking the assembling of ourselves together, as the manner of some is; but exhorting one another: and so much the more, as ye see the day approaching." (Hebrews 10:25)

But there are some things that are a little obscure. For example, one may know beyond a shadow of doubt that God has called them to full-time ministry. But is that to pastor, be a missionary or to teach in a Bible College? If I know that I'm called to pastor, then where?

These are questions that God can and will answer beyond a shadow of doubt. The details of

God's will can be obscured at times due to the many voices that demand our attention and the overwhelming needs we see in our world.

Some hold to the philosophy that the need constitutes the call. This is true for some within the context of their ministry. If one tries to respond to all the needs in general that we are surrounded with, we would spend a lot of time going in circles. Remember in God's economy there is the good and the best. God's will for each of us is the best. The best for each of us individually is determined by the talents, gifts and passions that God has given us. So the answers as to the details often come in response to an attitude of gratitude.

When we give God thanks for a prayer request before the answer comes, some surprising things happen. If you think God wants you to pastor in a certain location or to do something you believe to be His will, start thanking Him for opening doors to make that possible. One of two things will happen. You will receive stronger and stronger impressions that a particular thing is His will, eventually doors will start to open, miracles will happen, enabling us to do what we believe to be God's will. Or that particular impression will dissipate and be replaced with another.

About four years ago God put it upon my heart to start a foundation to work with disadvantaged families. He gave me a blue print that would address one of the greatest needs in our society. It will require a large sum of money to fund this plan, but it must be done. Every day I thank God for making this a reality. I don't know how He will do it, but He will.

I had the most amazing experience this past Saturday; an experience that only God could have orchestrated. I met a minister from Rochester, Minnesota. We shared some great fellowship. In the course of our conservation I shared my vision for this foundation. All of a sudden this big smile crossed his face and he said, "I know of an organization that does exactly what you just described." He went on to tell about the Jeremiah Plan, an organization in Minneapolis, Minnesota. They had contacted his church looking for people to work with in expanding their ministry into other cities. They have three locations presently.

This is amazing to find out about someone else who was following almost the identical blue print God had given me and has been blessed by God to raise the millions of dollars it takes to operate this kind of ministry. I'm not sure exactly how or when, but we will see the Jeremiah Plan at work here soon. Thank you God! Continue to thank God for the answers to prayer in advance.

Empowers us to, "Let go and Let God"

Developing a mindset of an attitude of gratitude will enable us to detach. There is a very thin line between attachment and detachment. But it is important to be able to recognize that line. It affects all of our relationships; in the home, with friends, at work, in the church and other organizations and our relationship with God.

We should be attached to others to a degree,

depending on the relationship. The more important the relationship, the more attached we should be.

The most important relationship is the family, but even in the family there will be a time and place to detach. To go beyond that line feels like control and manipulation to the other person. It can also feel like co-dependence and can lead to it in reality. This causes people to push us away, creating a chasm in the relationship. We need to detach before this happens. Having an attitude of gratitude in all things and for all the people God has put in our life will enable us to detach.

This same principle applies to our relationship with God. It is very important that we be attached to Jesus and God's written word, that we totally trust Him. But when it comes to the results of the work of ministry and prayers we need to detach. We need to leave the results of our work to God.

Often we feel that our prayer has not been answered, but in reality it has been. We are not accepting God's answer. Then there are times when God can't answer because we won't get out of the way and let Him answer. Remember God knows what is in our best interest and He always has our back. So, detach, get out of the way, or as has been said, "Let go and let God." Practicing an attitude of gratitude will enable us to get out of His way.

Manifest the Abundant Life

Developing a mindset of an attitude of gratitude will move us into the flow of God's blessings. "For as he thinketh in his heart, so is he: Eat and drink, saith he to thee; but his heart is not with thee." (Proverbs 23:7) "The outer conditions of a person's life will always be found to be harmoniously related to his inner state. Men do not attract that which they want, but that which they are." — James Allen, *As a Man Thinketh* ₂

We attract into our life what we think about. When we fail to be grateful by default, forgetfulness or on purpose, we harbor negative thoughts and feelings. Those thoughts and feelings can be anything from worry to resentment to bitterness to hate or revenge. Whatever they are, we can count on them to attract more of the same things into our life.

An attitude of gratitude to God activates thoughts and feelings of love, peace, joy and abundance. Gratefulness moves us into the flow of God's blessings and our life is filled with love, peace, joy and abundance. Give thanks in all things and expect blessings beyond your imagination.

Dr. Robert A. Emmons in his book, *Gratitude Works*, shares a document that was found in Sir John Templeton's personal archives. It was a short letter he had sent with his Christmas cards in 1962. In the letter he wanted the readers to think of their mind as a garden and themselves as the gardener.

"Circumstances outside the garden of your mind do not shape you. You shape them. For example, if you expect treachery, allowing those thoughts to dwell in your mind, you will get it. If you will fill your mind with thoughts of love, you will give love and get it. If you think little of God, He will be far from you. If you think often of God, the Holy Spirit will dwell more in you. The glory of the universe is open to every man. Some look and see. Some look and see not." [3]

Gratitude: A Strategy for Spiritual Warfare

Paul reminds us in Ephesians 6 that we are in a spiritual war and he instructs us as to how to be prepared in terms of armor, weapons and strategy. "Finally, my brethren, be strong in the Lord, and in the power of his might. Put on the whole armor of God, that ye may be able to stand against the wiles of the devil. For we wrestle not against flesh and blood, but against principalities, against powers, against the rulers of the darkness of this world, against spiritual wickedness in high places. Wherefore take unto you the whole armor of God, that ye may be able to withstand in the evil day, and having done all, to stand. Stand therefore, having your loins girt about with truth, and having on the breastplate of righteousness; And your feet shod with the preparation of the gospel of peace; Above all, taking the shield of faith, wherewith ye shall be able to quench all the fiery darts of the wicked. And take the helmet of salvation, and the sword of the Spirit, which is the word of God: Praying always with all prayer and supplication in the Spirit, and watching thereunto with all perseverance and supplication for all saints." (Ephesians 6: 10 -18)

One of the strategies used in military operations is to fool or trick the enemy so as to create confusion and doubt. This is one of Satan's favorite strategies. We see this all the way back to the beginning with Adam and Eve. "Now the serpent was more subtle than any beast of the field which the Lord God had made. And he said unto the woman, 'Yea, hath God said, Ye shall not eat of every tree of the garden?'" (Genesis 3: 1) Did God really say that? Are you sure He really meant that you could not eat the fruit of that one tree?

"And the serpent said unto the woman, 'Ye shall not surely die: For God doth know that in the day ye eat thereof, then your eyes shall be opened, and ye shall be as gods, knowing good and evil.'" (Genesis 3: 4-5) You won't really die. Don't you think God wants you to know the difference between good and evil?

Satan still to this day uses the same kind of trickery, trying to get us to doubt and question God. He also knows we are the most vulnerable to this strategy when we are tired and suffering from burnout. "And let us not be weary in well doing: for in due season we shall reap, if we faint not." (Galatians 6: 9)

"But ye, brethren, be not weary in well doing." (2 Thess. 3: 13). Paul warns us about becoming weary in our well doing because that is the time we are the most vulnerable to Satan's tricks. But Paul also gave us a strategy for defense against Satan's tricks when he wrote, "Praying always with all prayer and supplication in the Spirit, and watching thereunto with all perseverance and supplication for all saints." (Ephesians 6: 10 -18)

The prophet Isaiah also gave us a powerful strategy, "But they that wait upon the Lord shall renew their strength; they shall mount up with wings as eagles; they shall run, and not be weary; and they shall walk, and not faint." (Isaiah 40: 31)

We would like to add to this strategy some other words of Paul, "Rejoice evermore. Pray without ceasing. In all things give thanks: for this is the will of God in Christ Jesus concerning you." (1 Thess. 5: 16-18)

Waiting on God in gratitude, praise and prayer will renew our strength enabling us to overcome any burnout. It will enable us to avoid being tricked by Satan. We shall run and not be weary, we shall walk and not faint. We shall fly as if we had wings of eagles!

One of the few things I enjoy about flying is regardless what the weather is on the ground, if you get up high enough the sun is shining. I recently flew to Charlotte. It was gloomy on the ground here, but when we broke through the clouds the sun was very bright. In fact, you needed sunglasses if you were looking out of the window for a long period of time. That is the way it is with our spiritual life. Regardless how gloomy and hopeless things look here, God's Son is shining out there if we just rise high enough to see Him. Gratitude is the wind beneath our wings that enables us to live a consistent victorious life in Jesus.

These are just some of the benefits from an attitude of gratitude. As you continue your journey of gratitude God will continue to surprise you with His magnificent, unconditional love and grace.

CHAPTER SIX

Challenges to an Attitude of Gratitude

"If it doesn't challenge us it doesn't change us."
-Fred DeVito

Our Heavenly Father Always Knows Best? Remember the old TV series that ran from 1954-1960, "Father Knows Best."? Most of you haven't seen it, but some of you have. I'd suggest it would be fun for those of you who never saw it to watch an episode on YouTube. It is great family entertainment. One of the three children had a problem in each episode. Father solved their problem in twenty-five minutes and usually the child never knew he had anything to do with it. This is a great concept, but not true in our society today, sad to say. Many fathers today don't even know their children much less know what is best for them. But the one thing we can take to the bank is, our heavenly Father always knows best. He will always solve our problems and bring the best out of negative situations; however, He will often require more than twenty-five minutes. When this fact becomes part of the very fabric of our soul, it will act as a compass causing us to welcome all events in life with an attitude of gratitude.

If it Doesn't Challenge Us it Will not Grow Us

There are many things that will challenge us in developing an attitude of gratitude. Many people are ungrateful by default. They just never think about gratitude or the fact that there are so many things in life to be thankful for. They take all of life and everyone in their life for granted.

Then there is the narcissistic personality that feels all of life and everyone in their life is all about them. The number of people with this personality disorder is a very small percentage of the population; however, many of us have one or two characteristics of this disorder.

Then there are those who feel entitled. It is sad that our government is fostering this attitude. The result is more government control and less individual responsibility and initiative. But for those of us who see life as a gift and want to develop an attitude of gratitude there are still challenges.

The scripture says, "In all things give thanks." Quite frankly there are many things that happen in our lives that are very difficult to be thankful for. But remember God has our back. He loves us and has the perfect plan for us. He knows exactly what we need to become the person we were meant to be in this world and what we need to prepare for eternal life with Him. So, in everything that happens in our life there is a divine purpose. Even the experiences that are irritating, disappointing, and painful. If it doesn't challenge us it will not grow us. Through everything that happens, it is God's purpose to grow us.

In the rest of this chapter we want to share some stories that illustrate God's purpose in what we perceive to be bad or negative situations. Our situations are unique to each individual and our divine purpose varies, making it impossible to cover every situation. However, we hope and pray that these real life stories will inspire you to see God's purpose in your unique situation.

When Our Plans are Delayed or Changed.

We face many challenges to being thankful in all things, one of many is the fact that we want what we want when we want it. We plan and schedule expecting everything to go according to our plans. A good share of the time it doesn't work that way, just in case you haven't noticed.

When there are delays and/or we have to change our plans altogether we get upset. We worry, fret and sometimes may even become angry. We forget that God's time is not always our time. We forget to be thankful. But remember nothing ever just happens. There is always a reason. Often we aren't let in on the secret as to why we were delayed or had to change our plans, but sometimes

God lets us see the reason.

In the spring of '67 we were taking three teenagers from our Church in Michigan to visit Vennard Bible College in Oskaloosa, Iowa. We traveled across northern Illinois. We made a stop in the East Chicago area for gasoline, use of their restrooms, and drinks. As we prepared to leave, the car would not start. There was a mechanic on duty but he had just left for lunch, so there was an hour wait. We sat and waited, worried and fretted, very impatiently. Could the mechanic fix it? How much would it cost? Would it be okay for the rest of the trip? How long was it going to take? What time would we get there? Were we going to miss the activities planned for the evening, and a hundred other questions that the ungrateful mind could imagine. We could have been grateful that it happened at the gas station where there was a mechanic instead of being stranded along the highway. After thirty minutes I had this impression, "It will start now." I turned the key and the car started right up. (I drove that car for another two years and that never happened again.)

We got thirty minutes down the road and saw that a tornado had just passed through. It was an unbelievable sight, one I will never forget. Cars upside down, five eighteen-wheelers on their side in the right lane west bound, the same way we were going. They were lying end to end as if they were toys a child had been playing with and placed in a straight line on purpose.

Twenty-three people had died in that tornado. We could see a mobile home park off to the north that had been totally destroyed. If we hadn't been delayed we would have been right in the middle of that tornado. Thank you, God, for your delays.

Thank you, God, for your protection. Thank you for showing us the reason for the delay. May we be reminded in future delays that there is a reason; God may be protecting us from something. His timing is always perfect and He always knows best!

Life's Disappointments and Hurts

The following is Chelsea's story. Chelsea is a young Christian lady who has a dynamic faith and trust in God. Her love for Jesus shines through her life and conversation! Her story shows how God has our back in all situations. He knows what is in our best interest and His timing is always perfect. This is her story in her words. I wish you could hear her in person.

"Growing up, my father and I didn't have a very close relationship. He was always in and out of our lives. Being young I held a grudge toward my father. He rarely tried to get in touch with us four kids. He was in and out of jail. More in than out, from what I personally remember. Although I didn't have much of a bond with him, he is still my father. I don't know what all he went through, but I love him unconditionally through it all. By the time I was 20 years-old I knew I had to let my father know that I love and forgive him for everything. I wanted to find him. I just didn't know how or what to do.

"So, I went inside and wrote him a letter. I poured out my heart to him letting him know that I loved him and wanted a relationship with him. After I wrote the letter I contemplated on mailing it. Simply because writing it made me feel like a weight had been lifted.

"I didn't know what to do. So I asked my boyfriend what I should do. He said, 'Pray Chelsea, ask the Lord.' So, I called the dogs and we went outside. I found myself walking in circles, playing with the dogs and praying. As I was walking I had this weird feeling in my gut. I look down and there was what looked like a pretty cool rock. It was white with cracks filled with dirt. Something tells me to pick it up. Well, this cool-looking rock wasn't a rock, it was Styrofoam. I flip this little piece of Styrofoam over and it reads in capital letters, DAD. I fall to my knees crying and thanking God, the hairs on my arms standing up. He blatantly spelled it out for me. So I ran inside, called my little sister for my father's address. So, I sent the letter.

"Three months later no reply and we moved to St. Joseph, Missouri, four and a half hours away. Weeks later after getting settled in, I'm going on my everyday walk and as I'm talking to God, He tugs on my heart and causes me to want my dad. I again broke down crying on my knees begging God to let me know my father is alright and that he knows that I love him. I go inside and start searching online for my dad, looking up inmates and my dad's name and picture pops up.

"Wow, the emotions were unreal. I'm getting

his address, and it says he arrived in St. Joseph, Missouri at nine p.m. the night before. So, again God has shown Himself. He once again showed me what He can do and that He is with me.

"I get a hold of my dad and he sends me visitation forms. I quickly fill them out and turn them in. He calls me two weeks later to tell me that I have been approved.

"So, I drive 30 minutes to the jail and they tell me I have to change my pants. My jeans have holes in them. I found a dollar store and bought new jeans. When I got back to the jail, they tell me there is a problem with the paperwork and I can't see him today. I break down crying, will I ever get to see him?

"He is here waiting for a bed to open up in another location and could be moved anytime. I get back to the car and my boyfriend tells me to pray, 'His timing is always perfect,' Chelsea, 'just pray.' I dried my tears and prayed, thanking God for getting me where I am. I've been blessed to be able to talk with him and that's what I really needed. Maybe I'm not ready to see him yet.

"When we get home I check the mail. As I open the mailbox, I see a letter from my dad. I go to my room and start reading. I look up and say 'Thank you Lord, your timing is always perfect.'

"This letter from my dad had to be read before visiting him. I had to know these things before our visit, otherwise our visit wouldn't have been as special. My dad poured out his heart to me in that letter. I got to visit my father the following Sunday for four hours.

"We took pictures and caught up on life. It was the best visit I could ever ask for. God was with us and is still with us to this day. We talk and write each other weekly. He gets out soon and I get to start my life with him. Only God knows my future, but it's obvious He wants my father in my life."[*1]

Yes, God loves us, He knows us and knows exactly what we need, when we need it and He will provide it at exactly the right time. Thank you Chelsea for sharing!

Loss

Most of us at one time or another have experienced a situation that represented a loss in our lives. The loss of anything is accompanied by negative feelings. (We will address the loss of a loved one by death later.) But the scripture says, when we lose something, we should give thanks. Remember, God knows what is best and He wants the best for us. He knows that sometimes we have to lose something "good" so it can be replaced by the "best"; something that will challenge us and grow us.

My daughter, Tera, had an experience like this recently. She is a wellness coach and worked at this company for seven years. She was surprised when she received a thirty-day notice that her position was being terminated due to cutbacks. She had the option of a transfer or layoff. The transfer options were San Diego, California; Las Vegas, Nevada; or Cleveland, Ohio. Due to her family situation, she felt these were not viable options. So, she took the layoff. She prayed and thanked God that He would open the right doors.

Guess what? Before the thirty days had passed she had a new job, doing the same thing she had been doing, except it was a new program for this company. Instead of being one of seven or eight employees in that department, she is implementing a new program. She received a 30% increase in salary and is challenged by the opportunity to implement a program she believes in strongly. She had to move seventy-five miles from her previous home, but she has found the perfect home for her family.

She said, "I was getting too comfortable in my job and needed a challenge, but would have never looked for another job without being forced to." God always knows what is best for us and will bring it about, whatever it takes. In all things give thanks!

Loss of a Home

Emmons in his book, *Gratitude Works*, shares the following entry in the gratitude journal of Margret, a participant in one of his studies of gratitude journaling on gifts.

"A special gift today: as I was sorting out some papers, I ran across an inspirational clipping I had forgotten about: it tells about a man who was marooned on an island. Each day he prayed for rescue but none came. With much weary effort he built a hut to live in and to store provisions. Then one day the hut burned down. He cried out, 'All is gone. God how could you do this to me!' That day a ship came to rescue him. He said, 'How did you know I was here?' The reply was, 'We saw your smoke signal.' Remember that the next time your little hut is burning to the ground, it may be a signal that summons the grace of God. This clipping blessed me so when I first read it and now today, it mysteriously showed up to bless me again and to remind me again of how many times I've been rescued when I thought all was lost."*2

Yes, our heavenly Father knows best and will bring it into our lives even if it requires the house to burn to the ground!

Mental Pain

In experiences that hurt and cause us deep pain, we are to give thanks. In thinking of this I remember a story told by Dr. David Seamands in one of his sermons back In the '60s.

He and his wife were missionaries in India. While they were there they had a son, Steve. Steve was born with a club foot. They were a long distance from any city and medical facilities. The doctor told them, if they wanted Steve to walk without a limp, they would need to do therapy on the foot every day.

The therapy consisted of laying him on a table and bending his foot back in the opposite direction of the direction it was bent. As you can imagine this would be very painful for Steve. Of course his pain would cause pain of a different kind, for the parents. While Steve was too young to understand, he would cry, then the crying would turn into screaming.

When he learned to talk the screaming would turn into, "Stop it!" then to, "I hate you!" We can only imagine how that felt to the loving parents.

Dr. Seamands said, the only thing that kept them going was the words of the doctor, "You must do this if you want him to walk without a limp." Years later, Steve played tennis in college. Dr. Seamands said, "Every time we watched him walk off a tennis court without a sign of a limp, we thanked God that we continued the therapy." He went on to say, "Often in life I have found myself laying on my back looking up and saying, 'Stop it. I hate you!' And God would answer, 'My son I love you. I'll straighten the crooks and twists out of your life.'"*3

Thank God that He loves us enough to allow pain and the other things into our life that will straighten us and prepare us for eternity with Him.

This reminds me of Micheangelo and his sculpture of David. Someone asked him how he was going to do it. He supposedly said, "That is easy, I'll just chip away everything that is not David."*4

Our ultimate purpose is to be like Jesus. So God is chipping away everything that is not like Jesus in our lives.

The pain we experience in the loss of a loved one is probably the biggest challenge to gratitude that we can face. But even in that kind of situation we are to be grateful. The scripture says, "In all things." Some translations use "situation" or "circumstance" in place of "things." I don't believe God wants us to give thanks for evil events or sinful behavior of any kind. Every event in our life presents a set of circumstances and within those circumstances is a reason or reasons for gratitude. In some events we may have to search for the reason, but it is there. And remember God has promised us that He will always be with us and He will never give us more than we can handle. He has fulfilled that promise time and time again.

Loss of a Loved One to Death

When we lose someone to death, it is hard, if not impossible, to be grateful for death unless they have been in severe pain and suffered for a long time. In that situation we can often say and really feel it, "Thank you God that they are no longer suffering."

In other situations we have to look at it in terms of what that person has meant to us and how they enhanced our lives. We can recall meaningful experiences and be grateful for those experiences; how they enriched our lives and contributed to who we are. It doesn't take away the pain, but it will facilitate the mourning process. We heal only to the point that the negative, intrusive feelings that interfere with our normal activities and in some cases paralyze us, are desensitized. We can be grateful for memories and for the fact that God is with us.

Back in the mid-60's we had a neighbor who was a professed atheist. One day a nurse called from the local hospital asking me to visit my neighbor who was in the hospital. They had given her up to die. When it got dark she would have panic attacks and couldn't sleep until the sun came up. She had asked the nurse to call me and asked me to visit her.

I read to her the scripture passage of the disciples on the road to Emmaus. Remember how they were discouraged and confused and even though they didn't recognize Jesus at first they felt encouraged and enlightened as He spoke with them.

Then I told her I was going to pray and when I prayed Jesus was going to come and sit in the chair by her bed. (Those were words of faith.)

After I prayed, she said, "Roger, he is here!" She slept all night without calling for help for any reason. She accepted Christ as her Lord and savior the next day. She came home a few days later and never missed a Sunday in Church until she died a couple of years later.

She had lived with a fear of death and darkness all of her life. She would turn on all the lights in her house at night. She now shuts off all of her lights at bedtime. I share this to illustrate how real God's presence can be in our lives. All we have to do is call upon Him, even when hurting from the loss of a dear loved one!

I have lived long enough to see quite a number of my loved ones and friends die. I expect that family gatherings from now on will be more funerals then weddings. I'm not sure if there are more people here on earth that I would like to visit or if there are more over there with Jesus. It was kind of funny, I was thinking about this an hour ago walking across a Walmart parking lot. I almost got ran over. (I will go, of course, whenever God is ready, but I would like to finish this book first!) We experience every loss differently, but the mourning process is the same.

In 1972 I lost my father suddenly without warning. He was way too young, 54. I, my mother and five brothers missed him beyond description. I lost my rock, my security. After I was on my own I never asked him for any help of any kind other than advice. But I knew in the deepest part of my being, no doubt whatever, that if I should ever need anything he was there and would take care of it. I can't describe how real that knowledge was. It was just a fact to me. All of a sudden that security was gone. I was overwhelmed with a feeling of being totally lost: here on earth all alone. That is the kind of trust God wants us to have in Him. That kind of trust will enable us to give thanks in all things.

Even before Dad's funeral, my brothers and I were sharing memories of Dad and the tears of sadness flowed. As time went by whenever we got together we shared those same memories and the tears flowed, but they quite often were tears of joy celebrating Dad's life and rejoicing in the memories of him that had enriched our quality of life and played a big role in who we are today.

Of course we recall those memories at other times when we are alone. In fact, 42 years later I still recall a memory of something he said, did or even a facial expression he'd make several times a week. Forty-two years later we still do the same thing when my brothers and I get together (that is the ones that are left--in the last six years we have lost two brothers.)

We now have more memories to share. The

pain never completely goes away, but over time it moves from a ten to a one or two on a scale of one to ten. That process is greatly accelerated by recalling meaningful memories of time spent with the loved one, and giving thanks for the memories and the contribution that person made to our life. Thank you God, for the wonderful memories, what they added to our lives and the peace and joy they bring today!

These real events in real people's lives show us some reasons for being grateful in all things. Your situation and the lessons you need to learn may differ from these. I hope and pray regardless of how dark your situation may be, that through these stories God will inspire you to find reasons to give thanks in your situation. When you do you will be totally amazed at the surprises and growth our Heavenly Father has in store for you!

Always remember our heavenly Father knows best and He desires nothing but the best for us. He is growing us to be more like Jesus so that we will be a dynamic witness for Him here and preparing us to be comfortable with Him in heaven.

CHAPTER SEVEN

Gratitude as a Lifestyle

One dictionary definition of lifestyle is "The habits, attitudes, tastes, moral standards, economic level, etc., that together constitutes the mode of living of an individual or group." That pretty well sums up our objective for this journey of gratitude. May gratitude become the hallmark of our individual lives, our family, church and the touchstone for all of our activities.

Our journey in this book is close to coming to the end. But I hope and pray that your gratitude journey continues until that day. And that will be the beginning of a new journey of expressing gratitude and praise forever!

I want to leave you with some thoughts to motivate and inspire you to diligently continue your journey in developing a mindset of an attitude of gratitude.

Our Mind as a Garden

Dr. Robert A. Emmons in his book, *Gratitude Works*, shared a document that was found in Sir John Templeton's personal archives. It was a short letter he had sent with his Christmas cards in 1962. In the letter he wanted the readers to think of their mind as a garden and themselves as the gardener.

"If you exercise no control, it will become a weed patch and a source of shame and misery. If you exercise wise control, then it will be filled with God's miracles and become a place of indescribable beauty. You are free to choose which. How can you do it? Simply, for example, develop a habit of looking at each thought as you would a plant. If it is worthy, if it fits the plan you have for your mind, cultivate it. If not, replace it. How do you get it out of your mind? Simply by putting in its place two or three thoughts of love or worship, for no mind can dwell on more than two or three thoughts at one time. Circumstances outside the garden of your mind do not shape you. You shape them. For example, if you expect treachery, allowing those thoughts to dwell in your mind, you will get it. If you will fill your mind with thoughts of love, you will give love and get it. If you think little of God, He will be far from you. If you think often of God, the Holy Spirit will dwell more in you. The glory of the universe is open to every man. Some look and see. Some look and see not. Gardens are not made in a day. God gave you one lifetime for the job. Control of your garden or your mind grows with practice and study of the wisdom other minds have bequeathed to you. He who produces an item of unique beauty in his garden or his mind may have a duty to give that seed to others. As your body is the dwelling place of your mind, so is your mind the dwelling place of your soul. The mind you develop is your dwelling place for all your days on earth, and the soul you develop on earth may be the soul you are stuck with for eternity. God has given you the choice."[1]

What a beautiful analogy for life! And one of the plants we want to plant is gratitude. "Gratitude is not only the greatest of virtues, but the parent of all the virtues." (Marcus Tullius Cicero)

We Reap What We Sow

"Whatsoever a man soweth, that shall he also reap." (Galatians 6:7) However, some seeds come to fruition much sooner than others. The determining factors are the condition of the seed and soil. But regardless of the conditions, if the seed is nurtured and watered, it will come to fruition eventually. Some will experience their seed of gratitude coming to fruition very quickly and some may be like the seed of the Chinese bamboo tree.

The seed of a Chinese bamboo tree requires four to five years of nurturing and watering before it breaks through the soil. Can you imagine the patience and dedication required to grow a Chinese bamboo tree? But the good news is, it will reach full maturity the first year out of the ground, growing as much as eighty or ninety feet. Now that is a plant you could sit and watch grow. So, if your gratitude plant is slow to break through the soil, don't despair, it's just a matter of continual nurturing and watering. You will reap in due season, right on God's time table. And remember the best things in life are worth waiting for.

A Man after God's Heart!

What a testimony to one's life. Wouldn't you like that as an epitaph on your grave stone? Or even better than that, on judgment day hear God say, "Here is a man or woman after my own heart." That is what God said about David. "And when he had removed him, he raised up unto them David to be their king; to whom also he gave testimony, and said, I have found David the son of Jesse, a man after mine own heart, which shall fulfil all my will."(Acts 13:22) And Samuel referring to David, said to Saul, "Thou hast done foolishly: thou hast not kept the commandment of the Lord thy God, which he commanded thee: for now would the Lord have established thy kingdom upon Israel forever.

"But now thy kingdom shall not continue: the Lord hath sought him a man after his own heart, and the Lord hath commanded him to be captain over his people, because thou hast not kept that which the Lord commanded thee." (1 Samuel 13: 13-14)

We know David was an outstanding man. He was king of Israel for about forty years, a great leader and warrior. But he was a terrible sinner and had all kinds of family issues. He was just as human as any of us and perhaps more so than some of you readers. Jonathan Kirsch in the blurb on his book, *King David the Real Life of the Man Who Ruled Israel*, writes, "David King of the Jews, possessed every flaw and failing a mortal is capable of, yet men and women adored him and God showered him with many more blessings than He did Abraham or Moses. He was the original 'alpha male' and an authentic sex symbol, a ruggedly handsome man who inspired both hero-worship and carnal love. A charismatic leader, exalted 'As a man after God's own heart,' he was also capable of deep cunning and bloodthirsty violence."[*2]

Wow, it is almost overwhelming to think that a man like David could be called by God, "A man after His own heart." But by taking a closer look at David's life we can see the reason God called him, "A man after His own heart." In doing so we find hope for our own sins and failings. Much has been written speculating on the reasons God called David, "A man after His own heart." David had two outstanding characteristics that set him apart from many others, especially King Saul. First, he had a deep love, an unshakable faith and trust in God and His law. Secondly, he perceived all of life as a gift from God.

"David -- a man after mine own heart." That is, a man who would rule the kingdom according to God's will. Dr. Benson's observation on this point is very judicious: "When it is said that David was a man after God's own heart, it should be understood, not of his private, but of his public, character. He was a man after God's own heart, because he ruled the people according to the Divine will. He did not allow of idolatry; he did not set up for absolute power. He was guided in the government of the nation by the Law of Moses, as the standing rule of government, and by the prophet, or the Divine oracle, whereby God gave directions upon particular emergencies. Whatever Saul's private character was, he was not a good king in Israel. He did not follow the law, the oracle, and the prophet; but attempted to be absolute, and thereby to subvert the constitution of the kingdom." (Adam Clark)[3]

God knew David's heart, He knew David would rule Israel according to God's will. David proved his love and faith in God many times even as a youth. He showed no fear in protecting the sheep from the jaws of a bear or lion or facing the giant Goliath on the battlefield because of his faith in God to deliver his enemy into his hands. His faith enabled him to destroy mighty enemies on the battlefield. David was submissive to the authority of God, yet he was as human as most of us. He could identify with the apostle Paul many years before Paul penned the words, "For that which I do I allow not: for what I would, that do I not; but what I hate, that do I.

"If then I do that which I would not, I consent unto the law that it is good.

"Now then it is no more I that do it, but sin that dwelleth in me.

"For I know that in me (that is, in my flesh,) dwelleth no good thing: for to will is present with me; but how to perform that which is good I find not.

"For the good that I would I do not: but the

evil which I would not, that I do.

"Now if I do that I would not, it is no more I that do it, but sin that dwelleth in me." (Romans 7: 15-20)

We see this dilemma in David when confronted with the temptation of the fruit from the forbidden tree, Bathsheba. But we also get a glimpse of David's heart when confronted with his sin and the results thereof.

"And it came to pass in an evening tide, that David arose from off his bed, and walked upon the roof of the king's house: and from the roof he saw a woman washing herself; and the woman was very beautiful to look upon.

"And David sent and enquired after the woman. And one said, Is not this Bathsheba, the daughter of Eliam, the wife of Uriah the Hittite?

"And David sent messengers, and took her; and she came in unto him, and he lay with her; for she was purified from her uncleanness: and she returned unto her house.

"And the woman conceived, and sent and told David, and said, I am with child.

"And David sent to Joab, saying, Send me Uriah the Hittite. And Joab sent Uriah to David.

"And when Uriah was come unto him, David demanded of him how Joab did, and how the people did, and how the war prospered.

"And David said to Uriah, Go down to thy house, and wash thy feet. And Uriah departed out of the king's house, and there followed him a mess of meat from the king.

"But Uriah slept at the door of the king's house

with all the servants of his lord, and went not down to his house.

"And when they had told David, saying, Uriah went not down unto his house, David said unto Uriah, Camest thou not from thy journey? Why then didst thou not go down unto thine house?

"And Uriah said unto David, The ark, and Israel, and Judah, abide in tents; and my lord Joab, and the servants of my lord, are encamped in the open fields; shall I then go into mine house, to eat and to drink, and to lie with my wife? as thou livest, and as thy soul liveth, I will not do this thing.

"And David said to Uriah, Tarry here today also, and tomorrow I will let thee depart. So Uriah abode in Jerusalem that day, and the morrow.

"And when David had called him, he did eat and drink before him; and he made him drunk: and at even he went out to lie on his bed with the servants of his lord, but went not down to his house.

"And it came to pass in the morning, that David wrote a letter to Joab, and sent it by the hand of Uriah.

"And he wrote in the letter, saying, Set ye Uriah in the forefront of the hottest battle, and retire ye from him, that he may be smitten, and die.

"And it came to pass, when Joab observed the city, that he assigned Uriah unto a place where he knew that valiant men were.

"And the men of the city went out, and fought with Joab: and there fell some of the people of the servants of David; and Uriah the Hittite died also." (2 Samuel 11: 2-17)

When Nathan confronted David with his sin,

David didn't deny, make excuses or try to justify his behavior, but he immediately confessed, "I have sinned against the Lord." This was a confession of his sin as well as repentance and faith and Nathan responded, "Thou shalt not die." David was saved but it didn't change the effects of his sins on the lives of many people. However, it reveals that deep in David's heart was a love and submissiveness to the authority and sovereignty of God.

"And David said unto Nathan, I have sinned against the Lord. And Nathan said unto David, The Lord also hath put away thy sin; thou shalt not die." (2 Samuel 12:13)

We also see this in David's relationship with King Saul. God was displeased with Saul for his disobedience and had Samuel anoint David as the next king of Israel. David was very young at this time and it was many years before he would ascend to the throne. During that time Saul tried to kill David several times causing David to flee for his life and hide in the wilderness. There was at least two times that David had the opportunity to kill Saul.

"Then Saul took three thousand chosen men out of all Israel, and went to seek David and his men upon the rocks of the wild goats.

"And he came to the sheepcotes by the way, where was a cave; and Saul went in to cover his feet: and David and his men remained in the sides of the cave.

"And the men of David said unto him, Behold the day of which the Lord said unto thee, Behold, I will deliver thine enemy into thine hand, that thou mayest do to him as it shall seem good unto thee. Then David arose, and cut off the skirt of Saul's robe privily.

"And it came to pass afterward, that David's heart smote him, because he had cut off Saul's skirt.

"And he said unto his men, The Lord forbid that I should do this thing unto my master, the Lord's anointed, to stretch forth mine hand against him, seeing he is the anointed of the Lord.

"So David stayed his servants with these words, and suffered them not to rise against Saul. But Saul rose up out of the cave, and went on his way.

"David also arose afterward, and went out of the cave, and cried after Saul, saying, My lord the king. And when Saul looked behind him, David stooped with his face to the earth, and bowed himself.

"And David said to Saul, Wherefore hearest thou men's words, saying, Behold, David seeketh thy hurt?

"Behold, this day thine eyes have seen how that the Lord had delivered thee to day into mine hand in the cave: and some bade me kill thee: but mine eye spared thee; and I said, I will not put forth mine hand against my lord; for he is the Lord's anointed.

"Moreover, my father, see, yea, see the skirt of thy robe in my hand: for in that I cut off the skirt of thy robe, and killed thee not, know thou and see that there is neither evil nor transgression in mine hand, and I have not sinned against thee; yet thou huntest my soul to take it.

"The Lord judge between me and thee, and the

Lord avenge me of thee: but mine hand shall not be upon thee.

"As saith the proverb of the ancients, Wickedness proceedeth from the wicked: but mine hand shall not be upon thee." (1 Samuel 24: 2-13)

On another occasion David was presented with the same opportunity. "And David arose, and came to the place where Saul had pitched: and David beheld the place where Saul lay, and Abner the son of Ner, the captain of his host: and Saul lay in the trench, and the people pitched round about him.

"Then answered David and said to Ahimelech the Hittite, and to Abishai the son of Zeruiah, brother to Joab, saying, Who will go down with me to Saul to the camp? And Abishai said, I will go down with thee.

"So David and Abishai came to the people by night: and, behold, Saul lay sleeping within the trench, and his spear stuck in the ground at his bolster: but Abner and the people lay round about him.

"Then said Abishai to David, God hath delivered thine enemy into thine hand this day: now therefore let me smite him, I pray thee, with the spear even to the earth at once, and I will not smite him the second time.

"And David said to Abishai, Destroy him not: for who can stretch forth his hand against the Lord's anointed, and be guiltless?

"David said furthermore, As the Lord liveth, the Lord shall smite him; or his day shall come to die; or he shall descend into battle, and perish.

"The Lord forbid that I should stretch forth

mine hand against the Lord's anointed: but, I pray thee, take thou now the spear that is at his bolster, and the cruse of water, and let us go.

"So David took the spear and the cruse of water from Saul's bolster; and they got them away, and no man saw it, nor knew it, neither awaked: for they were all asleep; because a deep sleep from the Lord was fallen upon them." (1 Samuel 26: 4-12)

These two incidents give us insight into David's heart and his love and submissiveness to God's authority. He was not about to harm Saul because Saul was the God-anointed King of Israel. God made him king and God would take him down in His own time. And David was willing to wait on God's timing.

We also see in the scriptures that David was a man of gratitude. He realized that all of life is a gift from God even his anointing as King of Israel. The fact that he was a man of gratitude is inherent in the fact that he wrote half of the Psalms.

A Psalm is a song of prayer, praise and/or worship. Many of the Psalms are songs of praise. Praise is, "The offering of grateful homage in words or song as an act of worship." Based on that definition it seems that the Psalms of David reflect the heart of a man that is filled with gratitude to God. As an example consider the following:

"I will wash mine hands in innocency: so will I compass thine altar, O Lord: That I may publish with the voice of thanksgiving, and tell of all thy wondrous works." (Psalm 26: 6-7)

"O come, let us sing to the Lord; let us make a joyful noise to the rock of our salvation!

"Let us come into his presence with thanksgiving; let us make a joyful noise to him with songs of praise!

"For the Lord is a great God, and a great King above all gods.

"In his hand are the depths of the earth; the heights of the mountains are his also.

"The sea is his, for he made it, and the dry land, which his hands have formed.

"O come, let us worship and bow down, let us kneel before the Lord, our Maker!

"For he is our God, and we are the people of his pasture, and the sheep of his hand. O that today you would listen to his voice!" (Psalms 95: 1-7)

"Make a joyful noise unto the LORD, all ye lands.

"Serve the LORD with gladness: come before his presence with singing.

"Know ye that the LORD he is God: it is he that hath made us, and not we ourselves; we are his people, and the sheep of his pasture.

"Enter into his gates with thanksgiving, and into his courts with praise: be thankful unto him, and bless his name." (Psalms 100:1-4)

We could use many other examples but these get the point across. David was a man of gratitude who faced about every challenge to gratitude that is humanly possible. His life was threatened by his King, one of his sons and many other enemies. He experienced guilt resulting from his shortcomings and sinfulness. God's promises seem like they would never be fulfilled yet he remained grateful for life and his God! May he be an inspiration to us to continue our journey of developing a mindset of an attitude of gratitude!

Prayer of Thanksgiving

God of all blessings,
source of all life,
giver of all grace:
We thank you for the gift of life:
for the breath
that sustains life,
for the food of this earth
that nurtures life,
for the love of family and friends
without which there would be no life.
We thank you for the mystery of creation:
for the beauty
that the eye can see,
for the joy
that the ear may hear,
for the unknown
that we cannot behold filling the universe with
wonder,
for the expanse of space
that draws us beyond the definitions of our selves.
We thank you for setting us in communities:
for families
who nurture our becoming,
for friends
who love us by choice,
for companions at work,
who share our burdens and daily tasks,
for strangers
who welcome us into their midst,

for people from other lands
who call us to grow in understanding,
for children
who lighten our moments with delight,
for the unborn,
who offer us hope for the future.
We thank you for this day:
for life
and one more day to love,
for opportunity
and one more day to work for justice and peace,
for neighbors
and one more person to love
and by whom be loved,
for your grace
and one more experience of your presence,
for your promise:
to be with us,
to be our God,
and to give salvation.
For these, and all blessings,
we give you thanks, eternal, loving God,
through Jesus Christ we pray. Amen.[*1]

OUR PRAYER FOR YOU!

As you continue on your journey to developing a mindset of an attitude of gratitude may you know that "Joy unspeakable and peace that passes all understanding," that is a gift from God in Christ Jesus!

NOTES

1. All Bible quotes are from the King James version

Preface.

1. Adam Clark Commentary, comments on 1 Thessalonians 5:18

Introduction.

1. Viktor Frankl, *Man's Search For Meaning*, English Translation by Beacon Press 1959

Chapter One.

1. Gratitude Quiz, greatergood.berkeley.edu/quizzies/take_quiz 6

Chapter Two,

1. Rodert A. Emmons, *Gratitude Works,* by Jossey-Bass 2013
2. Ibid

Chapter Three

1. S. Michael Houdmann on GotQuestion.org
2. Barnes on the Bible, notes on Genesis 1:26
3. *I Love My Attorney* Author unknown
4. Rick Warren, *The Purpose Driven Life* by Zondervan 2003

Chapter Four

1. Adam Clark Commentary, comments on 1 Thessalonians 5:18
2. The Power of Gratitude, www.Gratitudeseeds.com
3. Tullian Tchividjian, *One Way Love* by

David C. Cook 2013
4.   Story of the Tightrope Walker, author unknown

Chapter Five

1.   Robert A. Emmons, article titled *No Thanks*
2.   James Allen, *As a Man Thinketh* published in 1902
3.   Robert A. Emmons, Gratitude Works, by Jossey-Bass 2013

Chapter Six

1.   Chelsea's Story as written for this book
2.   Robert A. Emmons, *Gratitude Works,* by Jossey-Bass 2013
3.   Dr. David Seamands, from a sermon given at Asbury University Church in the early 70s
4.   Micheangelo, someone supposedly ask him, how was going to do David. He said, "I will just chip away everything that is not David."

Chapter Seven

1.   Robert A. Emmons, *Gratitude Works* by Jossey-Bass 2013
2.   Jonathan Kirsch, *King David The Real Live of the Man Who Ruled Israel* by The Ballantine Publishing Group
3.   Adam Clark Commentary, comments on Acts 13:22

Prayer of Thanksgiving

1.   Vienna Cobb Anderson from *Prayers of Our Heart* 1991

Suggested Reading

Robert A. Emmons, *Gratitude Works* by Jossey-Bass 2013

Robert A. Emmons, *Thanks!* By Houghton Mifflin Company 2007

Nancy Leigh DeMoss, *Choosing Gratitude Your Journey to Joy*, Moody Publishers 2009

Mary Jo Leddy, *Radical Gratitude*, by Orbis Books 2oo2

Tullian Tchividjian, *One Way Love*, David C. Cook 2013

Matt Chandler, *To Live Is Christ, To Die Is Gain* by David C. Cook 2013

Online resources on Gratitude

greatergood.berkeley.edu
health.harvard.edu
huffingtonpost.com../havinggratitude
gratitudepower.net/science.htm
gapsychology.org/displaycommon.cf
happierhuman.com/the-science-of-gratitude

P.S.

Thank you for reading our book! I hope and pray that you enjoyed it and that it enriches your life. I hope to meet many of you before our journey here ends. I would love to speak at your church or church group. We could do a "Day of Gratitude," or a "Gratitude Weekend," or any combination that fits your schedule. I also enjoy company meetings, marketing, retail or manufacturing. Gratitude makes a big difference in all areas of life.

I pastored for 15 years, conducted workshops and seminars for ten years as well as one-on-one counseling. For 17 years I was in marketing. Three years ago I started doing some voice-over work, mostly audio books. At the present time I have 15 books on audible.com; this one will soon be the 16th. But my first love is public speaking and teaching. That is my strongest gift and greatest passion, especially the subject of gratitude.

If I can be of assistance contact me at rgrayvoice@gmail.com or voice-plus@Weebly.com or call me at 417-536-7801.